SHORT CUTS

OTHER TITLES IN THE SHORT CUTS SERIES

THE HORROR GENRE: FROM BEELZEBUB TO BLAIR WITCH
Paul Wells

THE STAR SYSTEM: HOLLYWOOD'S PRODUCTION OF POPULAR IDENTITIES
Paul McDonald

SCIENCE FICTION CINEMA: FROM OUTERSPACE TO CYBERSPACE
Geoff King and Tanya Krzywinska

EARLY SOVIET CINEMA: INNOVATION, IDEOLOGY, AND PROPAGANDA
David Gillespie

READING HOLLYWOOD: SPACES AND MEANINGS IN AMERICAN FILM
Deborah Thomas

DISASTER MOVIES: THE CINEMA OF CATASTROPHE
Stephen Keane

NEW CHINESE CINEMA: CHALLENGING REPRESENTATIONS
Sheila Cornelius

THE WESTERN GENRE

FROM LORDSBURG TO BIG WHISKEY

JOHN SAUNDERS

WALLFLOWER

LONDON and NEW YORK

A Wallflower Paperback

First published in Great Britain in 2001 by Wallflower Press
5 Pond Street, Hampstead, London NW3 2PN
www.wallflowerpress.co.uk

All stills courtesy of BFI Films: Stills, Posters and Designs
Used by permission

A catalogue record for this book is available from the British Library

ISBN 1 903364 12 4

Book Design by Rob Bowden Design

Printed in Great Britain by Biddles Limited, Guildford and King's Lynn

CONTENTS

LIST OF ILLUSTRATIONS

For Anna, Nicholas and Daniel

INTRODUCTION

This book investigates the continuing appeal of the western, the kinds of stories it tells, and the way it tells them. The introduction is concerned with distinctions and definitions and with the origins of a form which preceded the cinema by more than a century, though the new medium quickly seized on the visual and dramatic possibilities of this long tradition of tales and between the early years of the twentieth century and the mid-1970s literally thousands of western movies were made. The sheer scale of the genre makes it possible in this in brief study to discuss only a tiny sample of films. Our story will begin in 1939, the year which saw a revival of interest in the western by the major Hollywood studios, when John Ford sent his stagecoach over the floor of Monument Valley towards Lordsburg with John Wayne and the US Cavalry in attendance. Although that journey towards civilisation and safety was perilous, by 1939 the cultural assumptions behind it were easily recognised, the characters and situations long familiar.

Chapter 1 involves a detailed case study of *Shane* (1953), a film in which it has been said 'the legend of the West is virtually reduced to its essentials and then fixed in the dreamy clarity of a fairy tale' (Warshow 1954: 44). Our study of this influential film spells out some of the situations and assumptions peculiar to the genre.

Chapter 2 focuses on key works by three of the commanding figures of the western – John Ford, Howard Hawks and Anthony Mann – in the years when the genre was at its most popular and featured box-office stars such as John Wayne, James Stewart and Henry Fonda. Their quite dissimilar personae remind us that however formulaic the role of the hero and the models of masculinity displayed, there is room for a rich diversity of effect. Likewise, the consideration of three undoubted *auteurs* allows us to gauge how the genre may be inflected even in its most classical manifestations.

Development and change are then approached diachronically. In Chapter 3, the outlaw story, one of the staples of the western – in this case that of Jesse James (1847–82) as told over 40 years – is examined in sharply contrasting versions by Henry King, Philip Kaufman and Walter Hill. In Chapter 5, the encounter with the 'Indians' – from the 1950s increasingly problematic for the liberal sentiments of some of the film-makers – is illustrated with examples from Arthur Penn, Robert Aldrich and Kevin Costner.

Chapter 4 looks at the reawakening of interest in the genre in the early 1960s – often seen as a result of the impact of the spaghetti westerns following a period of relative decline, and the emergence of Sam Peckinpah, the director who, after Ford, has been most closely associated with the cowboy picture. His only real rival in this arena is Clint Eastwood, whose most recent western, *Unforgiven* (1992), is included here in the final chapter. Eastwood's hero, Will Munny, is drawn to Big Whiskey to redress the wrongs suffered by a woman at the hands of an unsympathetic community, but he is worlds away from Wayne's embodiment of the Ringo Kid, back in *Stagecoach* (1939). Far from defending 'the purity of his own image – in fact his honour' (Warshow 1954: 38), he works for a fistful of dollars in a more cynical age, and that image is remorselessly deconstructed. The picture is not quite so simple; Lordsburg was never the promised land, and Dallas and Ringo will move on, 'saved from the blessings of civilisation'. By the 1990s there is no place to go and Will simply disappears, 'some said to San Francisco, where it was rumoured he prospered in dry goods'.

Art or entertainment?

The early film-makers inherited not only a series of events but their re-enactment as entertainment. The western already existed, even beyond the

United States, as literature in the dime novels contemporaneous with the events themselves, wherein figures such as Buffalo Bill Cody were exploited as living legends, and as spectacle in the Wild West shows and still-popular rodeos. The literary antecedents of the form would have to include James Fenimore Cooper's 'Leather-Stocking' novels (1823–41), set on the north-west frontier in his own up-state New York and blending the oppositions and archetypes of European romance with specifically American settings and situations. Natty Bumppo, the white hunter and his lifelong companion Chingachgook, the last of the Mohicans, are both descendants of Homeric stories of friendship and forerunners of the Lone Ranger and Tonto. In his treatment of the Indian, Cooper draws on historical actuality, a romantic philosophy of nature, and the concept of the noble savage which predates Rousseau by more than a hundred years. His response to the indigenous American involves the 'splitting' often found in Hollywood's depiction of the Indian, with the cruel and treacherous Magua balanced by the faithful Uncas, given to the stately utterance heard from scores of his cinematic successors. Indeed, 'The Last of the Mohicans' was among the earliest stories to be taken up by the new medium, and the stereotypes already had the potential for a complexity often denied to the familiar formulae.

As early as 1908 reviewers of western films were complaining that it had all been done before and done better. This introduction does not aspire to the comprehensiveness that led Jon Tuska, when preparing *The Filming of the West* (1976) to view some 8,000 films. His book, like *The Western Film: From Silents to the Seventies* (Fenin and Everson (1977)), is there to be consulted, although it is often hard to see the wood for the trees. There were large-scale action movies – like *The Covered Wagon* (1923) and Fox's answer from the newly-signed John Ford, *The Iron Horse* (1924) (involving 5,000 extras) or films based on the writings of particular novelists, like Zane Grey, produced in the 1920s at Paramount. Others revolved around the early stars – Fred Thompson, Buck Jones, Hoot Gibson and the rest – or the star might be a dog, with Rin-tin-tin dominating this sub-genre from the mid-1920s until his death in 1932. The arrival of sound brought some problems, as did the Depression of 1929, but westerns survived and flourished, if often in the form of 'B' movies. New stars continued to appear – among

3

them Gene Autry in 1935 – to present a new, non-virile image: the singing cowboy, the nadir of the genre in many opinions (although it is useful to examine Peter Stanfield's essay 'Dixie Cowboys and Blue Yodels' in Buscombe and Pearson (1998) for a contextualisation of the phenomenon). John Wayne also appeared in this era, although he had to wait until 1939 and *Stagecoach* for recognition.

Stagecoach was Ford's first sound western, and for French film critic André Bazin it was already 'the ideal example of the maturity of a style brought to classic perfection' (1971: 149). By then everyone seemed clear what a western was, even if the obvious answer – a film about the west – is a shade tautological. The west – as a geographical area (roughly west of the Mississippi River and north of the Rio Grande) at a particular time (roughly from the end of the Civil War to the turn of the twentieth century) – makes sense as a point of reference, allowing one to categorise as pre-westerns Cooper's novels or *Drums Along the Mohawk* (1939), Ford's first colour picture, set before the War of the Revolution. 'Post-westerns' may be set well into the twentieth century, and often seem to involve Paul Newman in blue jeans, driving around in a pick-up truck. As Buscombe notes (1988: 16), a change in the means of transport marks one of the limits of the genre. The passage of time means that the films can look back, with nostalgia or bitterness, adding new themes to the standard repertory.

In 1959 eight of the ten top-rated shows on American television were westerns, while in Britain series like *Gunsmoke* commanded peak-time viewing. True, television had already killed off the low-budget 'B' pictures which 20 years earlier had kept 30 stars in regular employment, each turning out eight films a year, but John Cawelti (1971: 2) calculated that in 1958 54 feature-length westerns were released, using new extravagances of splendour and spectacle to get the customers back into the cinema. A down-turn in the early 1960s was reversed by the unexpected success of the 'spaghettis', the bastard Italian offspring lending the ageing progenitor a new lease of life. Yet although some of the most bankable actors of the period appeared in these films – Marlon Brando, Paul Newman, Robert Redford and Jack Nicholson among them – they do not come most readily to mind under a Stetson hat, and perhaps Clint Eastwood was the last major star to make his reputation through the western.

Just over a decade ago, in introducing *The BFI Companion to the Western* (Buscombe (1988)), Richard Schickel took its encyclopaedic ambitions as proof that the western genre was dead, the end of the trail finally marked off by a fat tombstone of a book. Yet the western refused to stay decently buried; *Dances with Wolves* (1990) and *The Last of the Mohicans* (1992) both drew the crowds, while Clint Eastwood's *Unforgiven* won the 1993 Oscars for Best Picture and Best Director and was surely evidence of more than his own enduring popularity. Other films followed, enabling Jim Kitses to identify a 'second wave' of revisionist westerns in the 1990s (Kitses & Rickman 1999). Even the gunfight at the OK Corral was revisited, twice in quick succession, in big-budget versions by George P. Cosmatos (*Tombstone* (1993)) and Lawrence Kasdan (*Wyatt Earp* (1994)).

History or Myth?

To return to the beginning, since movement was the distinguishing characteristic of the new cinematic medium, it is easy to see why the open-air shooting and absence of sound should favour the genre, with its emphasis on landscape, fights, and chases. It is unsurprising that Edwin S. Porter's *The Great Train Robbery* (1903) has a claim as one of the first narrative films of any kind. Like many westerns it drew on real events – a raid on a Union Pacific train three years before by the Hole-in-the-Wall gang (Butch Cassidy's bunch) – and other episodes in American history which recur in countless films – like Custer's Last Stand or the gunfight at OK Corral – which were less remote than the Second World War is from us today. When John Ford came to make *My Darling Clementine* in 1946, the story goes that he was able to draw on the details provided by Earp himself over a bottle of whiskey.

Western writer Frank Grüber is often quoted to the effect that there are only seven basic plots: the Cavalry and Indians story; the Union Pacific or Pony Express story; the Homesteaders or Squatters theme; the Cattle

Empire story; the Lawman story; the Revenge story; and the Outlaw story (Cawelti 1971: 34–5). Some of these clearly derive from a precise place and time, like the cattle drives up to the rail heads (such as Abilene) which appear in so many films – with *Red River* (1948) the most distinguished example – but which took place over less than a decade after the Civil War. Others can as readily be encountered outside the genre, so that the durability of the form is sometimes explained by its ability to digest and shape almost any source material. At the time of his death in 1967, Anthony Mann was apparently planning a new western, *King* – in fact a version of *King Lear*, and one can see how the tyrranical father figure and the rival brothers chime with the Oedipal preoccupations of Mann's completed westerns, although it would be surprising if the director had kept the three daughters. Yet it does appear that some kinds of thematic material are more appropriate for the western than others and there have been attempts to analyse this material and to account for its power.

At some point most introductions to the western allude to the historian Frederick Jackson Turner's 1893 lecture on 'The Significance of the Frontier in American History', in which he argued that the striking characteristics of the American intellect – restless energy, practical expediency, exuberance, and individualism among them – are the product of the highly charged encounter between civilisation and the wilderness, East and West: the frontier experience which lies behind so many western films. Whatever the validity of Turner's thesis, it represents what Americans would like to believe and so becomes available to the film-maker, and with the growth of American studies generally, to the film theorist and historian. After Bazin's pioneering efforts in the 1940s, the critics of *Cahiers du Cinéma* addressed the popular cinema with a new seriousness, discovering a coherent body of thematic concerns in the work of directors – or *auteurs* as they now became – such as Ford, Hawks and Mann. On the other side of the Atlantic, Andrew Sarris extended the canon, and on both during the 1960s the *auteur* theory developed a more rigorously systematic approach in place of mere biographical impressionism, drawing on the increasingly fashionable science of structuralism, with its basis in semiotics. Peter Wollen's *Signs and Meaning in the Cinema* sums up this new emphasis on patterns and motifs as 'indispensable for the critic' (Wollen 1969: 80) and takes the work of Howard Hawks as a test case. In the same year, Jim Kitses' influential *Horizons West* (1969) brings together the *auteur* theory and a structuralist analysis of the constituent elements of the form, organising the oppositions which generate its dramatic tension under the two headings of 'Wilderness' and 'Civilisation', Kitses draws on historian Henry Nash Smith's *Virgin Land: The American West as Symbol and Myth* (1950), a seminal work which had acknowledged the power of Turner's thesis and its definition of the frontier as the meeting point between savagery and civilisation, and even quoted Buffalo Bill Cody in support: 'I stood between savagery and civilisation most all my early days' (Nash Smith 1950: 119). The garden and the desert thus become available as concepts within film studies, particularly in the evolution of Ford's westerns, as we shall see. Nash Smith's understanding of myth as involving collective representations, rather than empirical fact, helps explain why the structural anthropology of Claude Levi-Strauss, developed to understand the function and significance of tribal myths, and along with linguistics another of the sources of structuralism, might be relevant too. What remains one of the most provocative studies of the western, Will Wright's *Sixguns and Society* (1975), admits its indebtedness to this work both for inspiration and methodology.

Four years earlier John G. Cawelti, in *The Six-Gun Mystique* (1971), had already published a more subtle synthesis of sociological and psychological insights in the search for a generalising concept, developing the idea of formula as an alternative to myth to describe the mixture of convention and invention on which popular art depends: 'A formula is a conventional system for structuring cultural products' (1971: 31). For the western, the formula is made up of settings and situations like those on Grüber's list, and involves characters – townspeople, outlaws, Indians, heroes and so on – to be introduced in the next section.

No doubt the collaborative nature of the medium and the scale of the production (remember those 30 stars each making eight pictures a year, (see Fenin and Everson 1977: 225)) account for the highly formulaic results, discouraging the search for a personal signature; the invention that operates in conjunction with the conventions. Thus, for Robin Wood (1968) *Rio*

Bravo (1959) shows Howard Hawks at his most personal and individual yet is the most traditional of films. In Chapter 2 there will be the opportunity to consider it alongside equally characteristic works by Ford and Mann to tease out the apparent paradox.

The past half-century has seen a proliferating body of criticism in which the western, along with the other major Hollywood genres, has been subjected to ever more sophisticated analysis. The 1990s made a distinctive contribution, as theoretical approaches developed on other forms were belatedly extended to the western. Gender and specatatorship in particular are singled out by Douglas Pye in *The Movie Book of the Western* (Cameron and Pye 1996), itself a testament to this new wave of critcism, while the subtitle of another recent study, *Westerns: Making the Man in Fiction and Film* (Mitchell 1996) underlines the point. In 'Postmodernism and the Western', his introduction to a still more recent collection, Jim Kitses suggests that 'to varying degrees, we are all auteurist, genre, formalist and ideological critics now' (Kitses & Rickman 1998: 27). No single approach will fit all films, and the readings that follow will draw on whichever promises to be most productive.

Definitions and distinctions

Cawelti's sense of formula as a cultural product and Wright's definition of myth as 'a communication from society to its members' (1975: 16), the embodiment of social meaning rather than personal message, promises a useful approach to a species of entertainment which in practice is usually experienced communally and in ignorance of a particular author. The language of such a communication will be open to formal analysis, and the significance of what is communicated will call for some understanding of the society which produces and receives the message. Although we are sometimes invited to see even the most apparently individualistic creative expression as ideologically determined, the terminology appropriate to such a view seems less plausible when discussing a lyric poem, for example, than when applied to the product of the Hollywood studios, large-scale capitalist enterprises dependent on a hard-headed calculation of market forces. If, as T. S. Eliot claimed, the truly original artist creates the taste by which he is enjoyed, then there is little originality in the Hollywood cinema, where the sense of what works for the audience in the collective memory of the film-makers or the horse sense of the moguls who managed them can only be modified and extended.

It has been argued that all film genres, in their conformity to previous models and the unvarying nature of the plot and characters, are essentially conservative, allowing vicarious experience of anti-social behaviour while inevitably vindicating the status quo. Certainly there are problems for genre theory in accommodating change if the form is only definable by a series of fixed relations, or Bazin's once-and-for-all classical perfection. Wood, like many other students of the western, has reservations about Fred Zinnemann's *High Noon* (1952), a popular and in many ways distinguished picture which the screenwriter Carl Foreman consciously presented as an allegory of McCarthyism. Wood's objections are to the contrived and unconvincing nature of the film, to how it does what it does, and Warshow is unhappy with the whole attempt to bend the traditional form to the requirements of a modern 'social drama' (1954: 44). More pithily, John Wayne pronounced it positively 'un-American' (Wills 1998: 347). The danger with Warshow's definition of the westerner, in one of the most seductive essays on the genre, is that in stressing the self-contained nature of the drama he excludes a potentially fruitful relationship with changes in the society outside. These changes must account for some of the developments in attitudes to the outlaw, outlined in Chapter 3, and to Native Americans, the subject of Chapter 5.

Yet even Wood, when writing of the ending of *Red River*, can describe Hawks as 'breaking the rules' (1968: 125) – and such rules exist, whether at the level of unconscious consensus or explicit guidelines within the process of production. Breaking them, as when Hawks avoids the threatened shoot-out between John Wayne and Montgomery Clift for a more benign conclusion, can bring new freedoms, but depends on the audience's familiarity with the conventions of the genre.

These conventions, as Edward Buscombe suggests in his useful essay 'The Idea of Genre in the American Cinema', borrowing from Wellek and

Warren's *Theory of Literature* (1949), can be categorised on the basis of outer and inner form. Outer form includes the visual aspects of the story: the setting, the costumes, the props – the most obvious definers of the genre. The inner form includes the stories and the larger historical and moral assumptions behind them – the 'idea' of the west as developed by Turner, Nash Smith and others. Will Wright classifies the film-makers' handling of this material under four headings: the classical plot; the vengeance variation; the transitional theme; and the professional plot, basing his analysis on the 64 most commercially successful westerns between 1930 and 1972. He arrives at this classification by distinguishing a number of elements or functions, describing the interaction between the characters, which make up each of these plots. They include situations familiar to the most casual observer: 'the villains endanger a friend of the hero' for instance (1975: 46), or 'a representative of society asks the hero to give up his revenge' (1975: 68). Moreover, Wright sees their combination in sequences not as simple concatenations of events but as explanations of, or at least as analogies for, social and economic change, articulating that communication from society to its members which is his definition of myth. This is not the place for a full consideration of Wright's ambitions, and objections will readily suggest themselves to his somewhat reductive emphasis on plot and economics, but it is an example of the way in which related disciplines can be brought to bear on the study of film.

The settings of the western are more than just background to the action; as Cawelti points out, again recalling Turner's hypothesis, it is 'a story which takes place on or near a frontier' (1971: 35). Similarly, the hero is not simply a brave man, but as we shall see in *Shane*, one caught up in the defence of the community while sharing some of the characteristics that threaten it. The women too are rarely mere 'love interest', but embody the civilisation he must defend, or perhaps those aspects of it from which he wishes to remain independent.

The characters in the western are inseparable from their actions, and here again any cinema-goer could list the stock types. The nine occupants of Ford's *Stagecoach* neatly represent most of them: the incorruptible marshal; the comic side-kick; the crooked banker; the whiskey drummer;

the gambler, the drunken doctor; the 'good bad girl'; the Eastern lady; and finally the Ringo Kid, the outlaw hero. Unchanging stereotypes which, in the novel, would soon appear threadbare, acquire solidity and texture when embodied by performers who instantly convey a wealth of experience in similar roles. Most resonant is the hero, the focus for the values which animate the genre, although in recent films he figures less unequivocally as the 'last gentleman' of Warshow's 1954 essay. Yet that fidelity to the purity of his own image for which the righting of wrongs provides the opportunity, rather than the motivation holds good even in a changing world.

Inner and outer form, through long familiarity, have taken on what has been called an iconic force, whether one understands the term in a strictly semiotic sense or more traditionally as having, in Kitses' phrase, 'a latent ritualistic meaning' (1969: 25). A figure on horseback riding through high country, a typical scene from any western, cannot strictly be said to symbolise something, yet often such scenes engage us as fully as the more overtly dramatic action. We might remember Nash Smith's designation of a symbol as 'an intellectual construction that fuses concept and emotion' (1950: v). No doubt we respond to a complex of implications – freedom, solitude, grandeur – especially when our feelings are orchestrated by a suitably expansive theme on the soundtrack, and no doubt a detailed psychological account of such feelings could be given, but for the moment we are content with the image.

Since the western has had a life outside the cinema on the printed page one hesitates to isolate the visual image as the sole source of significance (see Calder 1974; Tompkins 1992; and Mitchell 1996 for the western in other media). It seems unlikely that any single criterion will cover all cases, and one has to turn to individual films. Arguments from too narrow an understanding of the genre tend to see films departing from its conventions as somehow failing to realise the potential of the form. Wright has problems in classifying *Fort Apache* (1948) and *She Wore a Yellow Ribbon* (1949), two Ford films which pass his box-office test for consideration, and André Bazin has doubts about *Fort Apache* and wonders if another Ford film of the 1940s, *My Darling Clementine* is not weakened by 'baroque embellishment of the classicism of *Stagecoach*' (1971: 150). Wright's commitment to a method of analysis through binary oppositions developed for the study of folk tale and myth, rather than the complexities of the nineteenth-century novel, may seem appropriate to the formulae of the popular cinema, yet it could be argued that the form may be at its strongest when the mythic character is still discernible, although in conjunction with subtleties which prevent the myth registering as cliché. Blurring of the archetype need not imply loss of power, but a density and detail which make the best films repay repeated viewing.

In Chapter 1 a reading of *Shane* sets out to illustrate the conjunction of realism and myth that has proved so seductive over the years, before moving on to suggest the development and variety of the form, and to represent some of the leading film-makers and performers. It is difficult to reconcile the need for brevity with a desire for more than a generalised survey, but twelve films have been chosen for special attention, although in passing many more will be discussed. Most will be familiar, and through television and video remain accessible.

1   READING A WESTERN

Given the difficulties of separating the genre as concept from its actual
existence in individual films we shall take an example which sets out to
distil this elusive essence. *Shane* (1953) is often remembered as the archetypal western, a self-conscious attempt to reproduce the familiar themes
and characters in a classically pure state. For our purposes it may be an
advantage that the director, George Stevens, had no particular track record
in westerns, nor indeed many claims to be considered more than a highly
respected craftsman, expert at producing a good return for the studio's
investment. *Shane* was to prove the most commercially successful western
of the decade. As such it qualifies for Will Wright's attentions as an example
of the 'classical' plot (1975: 33), and unsurprisingly, since the model is
derived in large part from Stevens' film, it fits its list of functions with some
precision, thus offering an opportunity to test the validity of his thesis.

In its construction and techniques the film is an example of the so-called
classical Hollywood style (see Bordwell, Staiger & Thompson 1985) – as
indeed are the majority of western films – a style to which Stevens remained
faithful until his last picture in 1969. The distinction between *auteur* and
mere *metteur en scène* can never be absolute, and no doubt detailed study
of his output would reveal consistent traits and preferences, but the voice
of the genre should be more clearly audible when encountered in a rela-
tively unmarked form.

Even the star of the picture, Alan Ladd, had made his name in other genres, and his good looks ('like a young Greek god' (Linet 1979: 31), as he seemed to Sue Lyon, his agent and later his wife) were not of the rugged kind the part might seem to require. Although Ladd was still coming second in popularity only to John Wayne in the fan magazines, Paramount were beginning to doubt his ability to recoup the kind of money they were spending on *Shane*, and his ten-year association with the studio was about to end. In retrospect it is difficult not to read something of the melancholy of his later decline (ending in death from drink and barbiturates) in his portrayal of the gunfighter who has lived too long and knows it.

A. B. Guthrie Jr's screenplay was based on the novel of the same name by Jack Schaefer, published in 1949, often using the dialogue verbatim. However, the changes he makes repay attention. Some of them are consequent on the different medium, so that the first-person narrative of the character who becomes Joey in the film gives way to a more objective viewpoint, but even so we see events through his eyes and the camera angles ensure that, like him, we look up to Shane much of the time. Schaefer's novel is expanded to include scenes so often central to the genre – most notably the funeral of the character who becomes Torrey, dismissed in a couple of paragraphs but which on film becomes an extended homage to John Ford.

It has been calculated that in the period 1928–1960 Hollywood films usually consisted of between 14 and 35 sequences, running from two to five minutes and averaging between 12 and 30 shots (see Bordwell, Staiger & Thompson 1985). *Shane*, in fact, has an unusually high number of separate shots, averaging 720 per hour, but in other respects is structured conventionally. We might divide the 118 minutes of the film into sixteen sequences, roughly corresponding to the sixteen chapters of Schaefer's novel.

Shane's arrival

The duration of the action coincides with the hero's presence, and so it begins with his arrival. 'He rode into our valley in the summer of '89', in the opening words of the novel. As the titles appear, we find ourselves looking over the shoulder of a rider, half in silhouette, as he comes down from the mountains into the frame. From the earliest days landscape has been one of the most expressive codes available to the genre, and the association of high mountains with lofty feelings and moral elevation was deeply rooted, long before the West was won. Effects of scale and perspective work both to suggest the subservience of the merely human to some larger, more permanent order and to endow the figures in the landscape with comparable stature and impressiveness. Memorable examples include the settings of several of Ford's westerns in Monument Valley, Utah, where the gigantic sandstone bluffs, often sharing the frame with John Wayne's equally craggy persona, create a truly monumental effect.

We cut to a pastoral scene, a buck drinking from a sheet of water, the snow-capped mountains behind rising through fleecy white cloud into a brilliant blue sky. The farmhouse, its chimney gently smoking, blends with the landscape. The next shot reveals a boy stalking the buck, a close-up of the animal succeeded by another of the boy, his shining blond hair fringed with leaves, an image of innocent freedom. Only those immune to the charms of young children in films could deny that the nine-year-old Brandon De Wilde gives a remarkable performance. In the *New York Times*, it was his debut that was singled out, a tribute no doubt to Stevens' sympathetic direction.

As the distant rider moves along the far bank of the river, the buck raises its head to frame him between its antlers, a shot which encapsulates the elaborately, even excessively, composed style of the film. The deer splashes off as the boy runs to warn his father, chopping wood in front of the house, and we recognise the strong yet agreeable features of Van Heflin. 'Let him come,' is his response to the boy, expressing the patient fortitude which marks his character. Our first close-up of the stranger reveals Alan Ladd, leaning forward slightly, the pose of one of the best known of his publicity shots. He has been called an actor with only one expression, and this is it, but as George Stevens is reported to have said: 'Show me an actor with one good expression and I'll be happy' (Linet 1979: 150). It is not the face in the novel, 'lean and hard', nor is this the costume, 'dark … of some serge material, patched and faded and topped with a soft black Stetson'. Yet Ladd's buckskins, fresh from the wardrobe department, do have the 'kind of magnificence' remembered by Schaefer's narrator.

As the dialogue begins, the music – which has unobtrusively guided us so far – fades out. Provided by Victor Young, it is typical of the genre, scored for full orchestra in a mainstream late-nineteenth-century manner, with the sound painting developed for ballet and opera, often drawing on folk tunes and popular song and incorporating ethnic instruments such as the guitar and harmonica. Here it is a gentle, expansive theme, giving way to the mingled sounds of animals and a strange crooning which we eventually discover comes from the house, where a figure passing the window proves to be Marian (Jean Arthur), the farmer's wife.

The roles allotted to women in the western are painfully circumscribed, and it is fitting that we should meet her indoors, the 'Angel of the House', leaving the outside world to men and their doings. The flowers on the sill and the curtains at the window testify to her aspirations to a finer life, and in this case a civilising function so insistent that it risks alienating our sympathy. She seems to hunt down her son's lapses almost as relentlessly as Miss Watson pursues the errant Huck ('Mr Shane, Joey'). The relationship between Joe Starrett and his wife involves both dominance and deference – 'you heard what my little woman said' – although ultimately, as the audience expects, the decisions are his. Indeed, the rare films which show women in stronger roles, such as Nicholas Ray's *Johnny Guitar* (1954), where Joan Crawford and Mercedes McCambridge leave tough characters like Sterling Hayden and Ward Bond repeatedly nonplussed, risk being dismissed as frankly ludicrous, somehow not really westerns.

The newcomer singles out the boy in words from Schaefer's original ('You know I like a man who watches things going on around. It means he'll make his mark some day'), indicating his own watchfulness and the habit of homespun philosophical reflection typical of the western hero, who is never simply a man of action. After further dialogue, with Starrett's hospitality conveyed by the proffered dipper of water, Joey cocks the rifle with which he had stalked the deer and Shane whirls round, reaching for his

gun. The momentary unease is dispelled by Marian speaking softly, if chid-
ingly, to her son, and he comes forward, offering to show the rifle, the
kind of simple but disarming gesture so telling in the cinema, and Shane,
preparing to mount up, modestly admits that he can shoot 'a little bit'.

So far we have watched about five minutes screen time, involving some
sixty separate shots, and a full analysis would have to mention those details
common to the language of the Hollywood film whatever the subject, and
which could generally be left to the editor. The decision, for instance, to cut
from Shane dismounting to Joey jumping down from the fence, the visual
collaborating with the continuous music helping to create the seamless
flow which preserves the narrative illusion.

The conflict explained – the threat from the Rykers

Voices calling offscreen – a recurrent feature of the film – and a descending
chromatic figure from the horns signal a change of mood and an increase in
tension, as Starrett steps forward to take the rifle from his son. 'Looks like
your friends are a little late,' he says, as a bunch of horsemen appear in the
middle distance. The Ryker boys come over the river, the camera lingering
on the horses' hooves ploughing up the mud and trampling the kitchen
garden, emblematic of their casual destructiveness. Two of them speak –
Morgan, then the older brother, Rufe – to explain their business: a new
beef contract means that they need the land where Starrett has staked his
claim. The stage is set for a version of Grüber's 'Ranch story', one of his
seven basic plots.

As voices are raised, Marian comes out of the house to join her husband
and son. Rather surprisingly, she is wearing trousers, an assertion of
independence perhaps, but it is tempting to read it as evidence that the
domestic routine with her husband involves some repression of her natural
sexuality (in 1953 conventionally expressed by overtly feminine dress). Even
so, with their backs to the wall they constitute the American family, united
against outsiders, and it might be suggested that the names Joseph and
Marian hint at a still more archetypal family. At this point Shane, last seen
preparing to leave, steps from behind the cabin to take their side.

Shane accepted – the meal and the tree stump

The transition from stranger to friend occurs less dramatically in the book, where Shane intervenes to prevent Starrett being cheated over the purchase of a cultivator. It could be that the price of an agricultural imple-ment lacked the necessary iconic power; in any case, the introduction of the Rykers gives the threat to the homesteaders a more concrete force.

After apologising for his earlier suspicions, and opening the breech of the rifle to show that it was in fact empty – another ritual gesture of submission, and for determined seekers for the sexual sub-text even a confession of impotence – at Starrett's wife's prompting Shane is invited to dinner and introductions are made. 'Call me Shane' – thus we learn the stranger's name. Over the meal Starrett's talk of farming leaves Shane visibly inattentive, while Joey cannot take his eyes off the gun hanging over the back of the guest's chair.

As repayment for their hospitality, Shane takes an axe to the recalcitrant tree stump with which Starrett was struggling in the opening sequence, and is joined by his host, an important scene in the novel occupying the best part of two chapters. In a thoughtful essay on differences between book and film, James K. Folsom notes the novelist's advantages in conveying the symbolic values which, on celluloid, emerge as 'merely two men prosaically sweating and tugging at a large stump in a field' (Pilkington & Graham 1979: 71). It is true that the filming of the scene, using accelerated montage cutting on each stroke of the axes to a vigorous fugal figure on the soundtrack, is a little conventional. Ladd, always in danger of being overshadowed by the bulk of Heflin – although the novel does call for a contrast between 'lithe power' and 'sheer strength' – takes his shirt off, unlike the other man, to give us the full benefit of his musculature.

Marian, in line with woman's dual function as both an invitation to idealisation in others and the voice of realism in herself, suggests they hitch up the team, but as any student of the genre could tell her – and as Starrett does – 'sometimes there ain't nothing'll do but your own sweat and muscle'.

Shane and Joey in the morning – setting out for Grafton's

We dissolve to Joey asleep, inter-cut with the buck of the previous day, feeding in the garden. Although the presentation of photogenic children and animals may call for no justification, something more is going on here. Through their contiguity in the opening scene, and through his buckskin shirt, we associate Shane and the animal; both shy visitors from the wild. Yet as its hooves tangle with the strings protecting Marian's vegetables we make the connection with the threatening Rykers of the day before.

As roosters crow and what we come to recognise as the 'Shane theme' surfaces on the soundtrack, Joey discovers their guest waking in the barn. The next scene shows that Shane has agreed to help out and we see him leaving for town with the wagon to pick up some fence wire and some 'sure-enough work clothes', leaving his gun behind. In the novel Shane only puts on his gun for the final showdown; until then it remains in his blanket roll, an emblem of concealed violence. In the film it has to be visible for his intervention with the Rykers in the second sequence and because, as Joey says, it 'goes with him': the western hero is essentially a man with a gun. The conversation between father and son finds Joey still fascinated by the weapon and introduces the choice between alternative models of masculinity. This is a central theme of both novel and film. Joan Mellen finds the whole sequence embarrassing since it 'rabidly endorses' violent criteria of manhood (1978: 22) but this is to pre-judge the issue. It is true of course that Starrett's own qualities are inseparable from physical courage, nor can one imagine the most revisionist western seeing it differently. John Ford's *The Man Who Shot Liberty Valance* (1962) – which raises the question more explicitly than most – shows that although James Stewart's Rance Stoddard may be no expert with a gun he can throw a good punch, and it is this, rather than his law books, which wins him respect.

The sequence ends with the arrival of another homesteader, Ernie Wright, and more evidence of the Rykers' attempts to force them to pull out. In an effort to rally the others, Starrett calls for a meeting at his farm that night.

Soda pop and the confrontation with Chris

A dissolve takes us to Shane's arrival in front of Grafton's store, with a background of imposing mountain scenery and apprehension in the musical score, with the muted 'Ryker' horn calls. Shane's purchase of new work clothes leaves him 'kind of pale' at the two dollars two cents they cost, and his arrival attracts the attention of Chris Calloway (Ben Johnson) who is playing cards with more of Ryker's men in the adjoining barroom. The 'new sod-buster' provokes the predictable taunts, although a brief shot of Chris watching appreciatively, but not disrespectfully, as Lewis' daughter tries on a new hat has already hinted that he may not be as bad as the part he is playing. When Shane enters the bar to collect the soda pop he had promised Joey, there is general laughter, followed by an open challenge as Chris throws a glass of whiskey over the new blue shirt.

At this point in the novel we read that 'every line of his body was taut as stretched whipcord, was alive and somehow rich with an immense eagerness', but none of this is visible in Ladd's impassive features. What tension the scene has is situational; Shane's face expressing neither fear nor any effort of self-control, almost as if he has put off violence with his buckskins. The store clothes, which retain their newness for the rest of the film, separate him from his past without allowing him to merge with his new surroundings.

The homesteaders meet at Starrett's – news of Shane's backing down

As Shane comes in out of the rain and is introduced, another latecomer – Frank Torrey – arrives to good-humoured teasing and a burst of 'Dixie' on the harmonica from one of the others. In the novel he is just a 'nervous, fidgety man' with a stubborn streak, but here his nickname – 'Stonewall' – and his Confederate background are functional in what happens later. Another homesteader, Henry Shipstead, is renamed 'Axel' and becomes a Swede, a change similarly prompted by the generic theme of America as the 'melting pot', healing the North/South divide and uniting the races in a common purpose. Ford's cavalry pictures are an outstanding example of this unification, with their diversity of ethnic and social types coming together under the flag.

Lewis has passed on the news of what happened at Grafton's, and Shane gets up to leave in the face of the scarcely disguised contempt of the others. In the next room, where she is reading him a bed-time story, Marian calms Joey's incredulity and puts him to bed, her compassion for Shane evident as he appears at the window, outside the warmth of the cabin. Romance is in the air as the harmonica next door plays 'Beautiful Dreamer', the theme taken up by the full orchestra.

Jean Arthur has a difficult role to play, and sometimes seems unsure of how much of a love story this is supposed to be. Several years older than Ladd or Heflin, this was to be her last film, and there is a muted quality in her acting as she alternates between a steady, luminous gaze towards her menfolk and her mildly harassed attention to Joey. True, the problems for the actress parallel those for the character. 'Did ever a woman have two such men?' Marian exclaims at one point in the novel, and the answer is probably no, not in the long term. We never really doubt her fidelity to Joe, and there is a limit to the time Shane can stay around without compromising his masculinity. In the event the problem is resolved by a separate operation of the plot: the arrival of Wilson the gunfighter.

Meanwhile, back at the ranch, Starrett and the other seven home-steaders agree to go into town together the next Saturday. In the next room, Marian seems to be speaking for herself when she tells Joey: 'Don't get to liking Shane too much ... he'll be moving on one day'.

The homesteaders' Saturday in town and the fight with Chris

Shane gallantly hands Marian up and the wagons roll into town, picking up other settlers on the way with shouted greetings and cheerful bustle; for the first time suggesting the sense of community which the homesteaders are out to defend. The beauty of the landscape, with the mountains behind as they take the trail alongside the river, is enhanced by a suitably *nobilmente* theme on the soundtrack, although a crash of thunder hints at trouble ahead.

As the homesteaders enter the store there is eye contact between Shane and the watching Chris, and once inside, more of the realistic detail which separates *Shane* from the run of 'B' westerns. We hear of plans for a get-together on the Fourth of July, partly to celebrate the Starretts' wedding anniversary. One sequence is generally linked to the next by this kind of preparatory information – part of the accepted language of the Hollywood film of the period. Joey is about to return the empty soda pop bottle when Shane intervenes. He enters the bar to the expected insults and Chris steps up to face him. Two whiskies are ordered and the first is thrown over Chris's shirt, the second in his face, followed by a punch to the jaw, sending him through the swing doors and into the store, where Mrs Shipstead faints. This is a comic touch which, like the wide-eyed presence of Joey biting on a stick of candy, converts what happens to spectacle, the bare-fisted settling of accounts familiar from a thousand westerns.

Shane and Starrett defeat the Rykers – Wilson the gunfighter is sent for

This sequence is pivotal. So far Shane's battle with Chris has been a matter of personal honour. "T'aint our fight,' Lewis comments as he and the others remain safely outside. Although Rufe Ryker offers him a job at double whatever Starrett is paying we never doubt Ladd's refusal, especially when Ryker hints that Starrett's pretty wife is the reason for his loyalty to his present employer, and confrontation is inevitable as he finds himself surrounded. Joey's protest ('Shane, there's too many') elicits the predictable response ('You wouldn't want me to run away?'), and the general mêlée begins.

Still the homesteaders refuse to get involved, a necessary *donné* of the formula since society must be weak enough to require the intervention of the hero, but something of a problem for the genre which does not want to show ordinary American citizens as cowardly and ineffectual – one of the criticisms levelled against *High Noon*. The problem is solved by the appearance of Joe Starrett as the representative of the best the community has to offer, with a pick handle and an exhilarating display of bullish strength.

More or less naturalistic camera set-ups give way to alternating shots of the two back-to-back or exchanging smiles of mutual encouragement, and music – withheld from the sequence until now – is heard, a jaunty triumphal theme which assures us of their victory.

While they head for home in the wagon with Marian and Joey, the bruised Rykers register the new situation in the bar, and decide to send to Cheyenne for a professional gunfighter, as we later discover. At the farm Marian dresses the wounds, her gentleness and the men's modest disclaimers counterpointed with Joey's admiring interruptions. Shane and Marian share a moment of lamp-lit intimacy – he uses her name for the first time – before she is called away to put Joey to bed. We stay with Shane, who overhears the boy's declaration that he loves Shane 'almost as much as Pa', and her agreement that he is 'a fine man', before tactfully leaving for the stable where he sleeps. As a new, rather wheedling, theme seems to signal this liking, Marian turns to Joe who has entered from the other door: 'Joe, hold me. Don't say anything, just hold me tight'. In the novel Joe does speak: 'Don't fret yourself, Marian. I'm man enough to know a better when his trail meets mine'. The two men seem to inhabit different areas of reality, or rather Shane represents a romantic dream which scarcely overlaps with the flesh-and-blood presence of Starrett.

Wilson's arrival and the attack on Ernie Wright's farm

A heavy *ostinato* theme accompanies a horseman riding towards Grafton's store. A close-up shows the high cheekbones beneath the black hat – Jack Palance, one of the most compelling performances in the film. As the novel has it, there is 'something of a dude about his clothes,' but the dark costume is not so different from Shane's in Schaefer's description. In opting for a simpler black/white opposition Stevens sacrifices some of the deliberate parallels between the two.

Leaving Wilson waiting to speak to Ryker, elegantly slouched against the stovepipe, indifferent to the day's celebrations (it is the Fourth of July), his stillness charged with menace, we cut to Torrey arriving at Ernie Wright's farm. The family are packing up after more trouble from Ryker's men in which his prize sow has been slaughtered. For all his big talk, Torrey is help-less. In the meantime, he plans to ride into Grafton's to collect some drink for the party.

The shooting lesson

We move to Shane, mending wire cut by Ryker's men, who taunt him from the far side of the river. Joey's questions elicit the customary soft answers as he studiously declines the heroic role the boy's worship proposes. Back at the barn, Joey reminds Shane of his promise to teach him to shoot and, after some reluctance, the gun emerges from the blanket roll. Once outside, the professional's enthusiasm for his craft takes over, and the instructions are verbatim from the novel, although there Shane's moralising has only the boy for an audience: 'A gun is a tool ... as good – and as bad – as the man who carries it'. In the film Marian arrives in her wedding dress in time to witness the startling explosion of force as Shane exhibits his prowess, to Joey's admiring whistle, giving the scene an element of sexual display.

A gun is indeed a tool, although its phallic power must be repressed if the asexual domesticity of the Starrett household is to be preserved. In arguing for the legitimate use of violence the scene is close to the heart of the genre, in which the point, as Warshow recognises, is not the violence itself 'but a certain image of man, a style, which expresses itself most clearly in violence' (1954: 47).

Marian is not persuaded by Shane's justification. 'Guns aren't going to be my boy's life,' she says. Summoned by the shots, Starrett rides up, embracing wife and friend in his happiness at the prospect of the forthcoming party, but it is his wife he shepherds through the gate towards the house. It swings to, leaving Shane excluded again.

The Fourth of July and the Rykers' ultimatum

We cut to the town as a gate swings open, releasing a bronco bucking to unseat its rider out into the street, where shouts and gunfire show that the

FIGURE 1 *Shane*

celebrations are under way. Inside Grafton's the Ryker brothers and Wilson
are in a different mood. Wilson sits silent, while on the soundtrack a muted
version of the *ostinato* theme which announced his arrival plays. Torrey
enters the bar somewhat nervously, but manages a show of bravado, ironically congratulating Ryker for running Ernie Wright off his claim. Elisha Cook
Jr's small stature has brought him many similar roles, doggedly biting off
more than he can chew. We read him as one of nature's losers and are
prepared for later developments.

The roar of a cannon, improvised with gunpowder and an anvil, takes us to the homesteaders' celebration at the Shipstead farm. Independence Day is also the tenth anniversary of Joe Starrett's marriage, and his stumbling reply to the congratulations ('no man ever gave up his independence as easy as I did') has a bearing on the genre's conception of the hero as a man apart. Yet marriage gives him a stake in life: he and Marian form a couple as they kiss, contrasted with the other pairing, Shane and Joey, relegated to the background. The hero's celibacy condemns him to a kind of immaturity; in this society where marriage is the norm he is an outsider. Ladd's pensive features show that none of this is lost on him, and Marian looks back as though interpreting his feelings.

Torrey brings news of Ernie Wright's departure, dismounting unsteadily from his horse to good-natured joshing and a brief snatch of 'Marching Through Georgia' on the harmonica, but for the moment the dancing continues. His description of the new man Ryker has taken on ('kinda lean – he wears a black hat'), almost comically true to the sartorial conventions of the genre, enables Shane to identify Wilson, a gunfighter out of Cheyenne, although he is guarded about the extent of his acquaintance. One of the functions of the classical plot, as enumerated by Will Wright, is that the society does not completely accept the hero. His lifestyle challenges their own, and they feel something of the resentment they have for the villains. Torrey, at least, is undeterred, and arranges to accompany Shipstead to the blacksmith's in town.

We cut to the Starretts riding home through the darkness, again with Shane and Joey taking a back seat in the wagon. Morgan Ryker meets them at the gate, and his brother has a new proposition to make: 'How would you like to work for me?' In the novel Fletcher, the cattle baron, has no brother, although one of his men is named Morgan, and it is possible to see the splitting of the role as adding an extra dimension to the opposition. Morgan has no redeeming features; his mirthless chuckle is a recurrent and disturbing sound and it is he who shoots Shane, in an ambush, in the final sequence. Rufe is the spokesman for the land's heroic – if lawless – past, telling how he and others like him defeated the Indians and the rustlers to make the range safe, only to find themselves cut off from their water by the newcomers.

Formally, of course, Wilson and the Rykers are simply 'the villains', as abstract a threat as the dragons and sea monsters of romance, but we follow the historical debate with some attention. Wright's reading of the classical western as a reflection of the market economy defines the big ranchers as not simply 'outside society' (1975: 132); rather they represent a self-interested acquisitiveness which is part of the dynamic of capitalist society, although often in conflict with the communal values which it claims to advocate. Their argument with the homesteaders is about the kind of society which should prevail. In fact the period which is reconstructed complicates the simple populist moral argument; history is not really on the Rykers' side.

Nostalgia for the open range is often balanced against the recognition of necessary change. In *The Man Who Shot Liberty Valance* the cowboys' champion has a name which suggests that his irresponsibility is not simply licence, and although Lee Marvin's characterisation of the role stresses the anarchic destructiveness there is also a childish naïveté which evokes other feelings. Significantly he can coexist with the traditional hero, Tom Doniphon (John Wayne), until the advent of the new-style hero, Ranse Stoddard (James Stewart) precipitates changes which leave no place for either of them.

Throughout the exchange between Ryker and Starrett, Wilson and Shane have been sizing each other up. Perhaps significantly, Wilson drinks from the water dipper as had Shane on his first arriving, another visual parallel suggesting affinities between the two.

Torrey killed by Wilson

A dissolve shows Shipstead and Torrey riding into town, with 'Dixie' on the soundtrack in a sombre key, juxtaposed with the familiar Ryker horncalls, and Wilson, seeing the chance to push matters to a crisis, steps out onto the boardwalk. As thunder rumbles ominously, together with the leitmotiv we have come to associate with Wilson, Torrey's nickname, 'Stonewall', is used to taunt him, and he eventually rises to the bait as Wilson dismisses Jackson, Lee 'and all the rest of them Rebs' as 'Southern trash'.

In the novel it is Ernie Wright, earlier described as 'so dark-complected that there were rumours he was part-Indian', who is Wilson's victim, responding to taunts that he is a 'breed', a 'cross-bred squatter'. Although other films of the period confront it, characteristically Shane avoids the racial issue, still uncomfortably topical, for the safely distant Civil War antagonism.

In spite of Shipstead's shouted warning, Torrey draws, but is easily beaten by the gunfighter, the impact lifting him off his feet and stretching him backwards in the mud. After the uneasy silence of the last few minutes, the gunshot and the apparent realism of its effect is startling. Shouted exchanges along the street construct the official version of the incident ('a sod-buster tried to kill Wilson') which Shipstead cannot deny. Again, 'Dixie' is heard on the soundtrack, this time with tragic emphasis.

The settlers' apparent defeat; Torrey's funeral

A dissolve takes us to Fred Lewis' farm, as the music swells with Puccini-like mounting chords, and the women emerge to hear Shipstead's news. We cut to the Starretts', where Joe's reaction is to go into town ('sooner or later someone's got to go') but Shane and Marian restrain him. Shipstead fears that the other homesteaders will leave now, and we cut to the Lewises packing up and loading the wagon. They agree at least to stop at Cemetery Hill on their way out, to see Stonewall get a Christian burial. We move with a dissolve to the street outside Grafton's, where the locals are listening to the hymns from the nearby graveyard. A low-angle pan takes us closer, as Shipstead leads the mourners in the Lord's Prayer. The carefully grouped figures against the skyline – Joe with head bowed but resolute and Shane a slighter but still upright figure – are redolent of significance. One remembers, as perhaps did Stevens and his cameraman, the funeral of Trooper Smith in *She Wore a Yellow Ribbon*, or the scene in another Ford film, *The Searchers* (1956), where Mrs Jorgenson declares that the new land can never really be theirs until the settlers' bones have gone into the ground. The moving camera picks out other signs which point rather to the future: Joey stroking a young colt and a little girl eyeing Joey. As the 'Last Post' sounds we pan to the right over the line of mourners in near silhouette against the blue sky, until jarring chords take us back to Grafton's and the problem still to be solved. The funeral begins to break up, while Joe makes a final effort to stop them, but sits down discouraged as the others make the expected objections.

At this point Shane speaks: 'You know what he wants you to stay for? Something that means more to you than anything else – your families, your wives and kids'. Taking fresh heart Joe gets up again and rises to new heights of eloquence: 'God didn't make all this country just for one man like Ryker.' The decision could go either way – 'He's got it though, and that's what counts,' Lewis ruefully reminds them – when we pan left to see smoke rising from the direction of Lewis' abandoned farm. Resentment catalyses a renewed sense of purpose, and alternating voices join in a chorus of offers of help. Explicit stylisation of the dialogue ('You'd do all that, just for us?') and a crescendo of increasingly affirmative music ends with the Lewis wagon heading back to save what they can from the fire with some of the others following. Joe promises that he will have it out with Ryker, 'even if I have to kill him'. 'That's wrong, you mustn't even think that,' Marian protests, leaving the moral dilemma starkly stated: only through violence can violence be countered. The flames from Lewis' farm and the sinister Ryker music underline this before we cut to later the same evening, and plans at Grafton's for luring Starrett in.

Starrett accepts Ryker's challenge; Chris warns Shane of the trap

We find Joe saddling up while Marian, Shane and Joey sit round the table, apparently powerless to stop him. Back at Grafton's, Rufe gives his brother instructions to invite Starrett to a parley. Morgan delivers the message, and we see that Shane has been covering them from the barn, and he is still there when Chris rides up and dismounts, with the warning that 'Starrett is up against a stacked deck'. He also announces that 'something has come over him', that he is quitting Ryker, and receives an encouraging handshake from Shane.

Although he has little to say about its meaning, Will Wright finds this sequence sufficiently prevalent in the 'classical' plot to warrant a separate category: 'there is a strong friendship or respect between the hero and a villain' (1975: 45). Partly it suggests a professional respect which unites characters apparently separated by conventional moral criteria, or at least by social prejudice, and in this instance operates as a further tribute to Shane's benign influence in helping others to discover their best selves.

Meanwhile Joe loads his gun. In spite of Marian's efforts to keep him, he cannot 'show yellow' to her or his son, and he knows that she will be taken care of if anything happens to him. Marian can only bury her head in her hands.

Shane and Starrett fight; Marian and Shane part

After a brief glimpse of both the Rykers and Wilson waiting at Grafton's – although Morgan had promised that only Rufe would be there – we see Shane back at the farm, saddling his horse. As announced by Joey, he is wearing his gun and is again clad in buckskins. 'Don't let him go, Shane. Don't anybody go!' cries the confused Marian, but Shane has made his decision: 'This is my kind of game'.

At this point in the novel Shane simply knocks Joe out with the barrel of his gun and leaves to keep his appointment with destiny. Here a fist-fight of heroic proportions develops out in the yard, while Joey and Marian rush from window to window to watch. It is tempting to see the fight as expressing the subconscious rivalry of the two over Marian, but difficult to feel that this is the case (as it is in the somewhat similar triangle comprised of Tom, Ranse, and Hallie in *The Man Who Shot Liberty Valance*), so thoroughly is the sexual element transmuted into feelings of mutual respect. Rather the sequence serves to establish Joe's strength in Joey's eyes – throughout the encounter drawn equally to both men – since he seems likely to prevail until Shane draws his gun and knocks him out. At this obvious unfairness, Joey's allegiance is decided: 'I hate you, Shane!'

although of course, like his mother, he soon understands that Shane did what he had to do.

Over the prostrate body of her husband, Marian and Shane say their farewells. 'Are you doing this just for me?' she asks. 'For you, Marian. For Joe, and little Joe'. Recalled to the reviving Joe by the boy, her eyes are still on Shane as he rides out through the yard gate, the night sky almost as blue as at his arrival and with the theme music again in evidence. What remains to be done calls for the hero rather than the domestic man.

The showdown with Wilson and Shane's departure

An establishing shot of the town with the mountains behind (looking rather artificial in the day-for-night process) is followed by another of the interior of Grafton's, the men restlessly pacing the floor. Morgan takes a rifle and climbs the stairs to the balcony. The next shot shows Shane riding along the skyline, suitably heroic music on the soundtrack interestingly alluding on the timpani to the *ostinato* theme usually associated with Wilson. In the novel the narrator remembers him as a figure of menace, dark and forbidding – 'he was tall and terrible there on the road, looming up gigantic in the mystic half light' – and the film conveys something of this effect. We see Joey and the dog run after him, taking the trail along by the river followed on the Saturday the homesteaders rode into town. The soundtrack is now openly aggressive, with dissonant, jagged phrases from the orchestra. Shane rides on, passing a formation of three birch trees often singled out in the preceding action. One stands tall, to the left of the frame, while the other two seem to spring from a single root, one vertical and the other at an angle of about forty degrees. We could perhaps read this as a symbolic statement of Shane's separateness and the crippled but still living relationship between the Starretts. Joey and the dog scramble on, over Cemetery Hill, an overlapping dissolve juxtaposing Shane and the shadowy crosses, until he nears Grafton's store.

Inside, the rich darkness is broken by the lighted lamps and the white sleeves of the seated Wilson, and the music fades to a regular *pianissimo* drum-beat. Shane moves to the bar and turns to Ryker, as Joey and the

72965

dog take up a vantage point underneath the swing doors: 'You've lived too long. Your kind of days are over'. 'What about yours, gunfighter?' Ryker counters. 'The difference is, I know it,' replies Shane, but there is still time for Wilson, who now rises to his feet. For once Ladd gets some steel into his bottom register: 'I've heard you're a low-down Yankee liar'. 'Prove it,' Wilson demands, as he had of Torrey. The gunshots blur, but the silence finds Shane still standing while Ryker and Wilson are dead, the latter grotesquely buried beneath a pile of collapsing barrels, as though Stevens were anxious to erase the dangerous glamour he has allowed him to assume. With a professional flourish, Shane returns his gun to its holster, before a sound overhead prompts Joey's shouted warning. He whirls round, draws and shoots in one movement, and Morgan Ryker staggers forward and topples over the balcony, bringing the rail with him as he crashes to the floor.

In the novel it is clear that one of Wilson's bullets has hit Shane, even before the shot from the balcony, a stain on his shirt 'spreading fanlike above the belt'. Here the wound is apparent only when Joey, at their parting, notices the blood at his wrist, and we assume that it was inflicted by Morgan. The hero is vulnerable only to deceit, although in opting for this mythic immunity the film sacrifices the extra irony of the book's sugges-tion that it is because he has tried to abandon his calling – that he is in fact out of practice – that Shane is not quick enough to evade Wilson's shot. Although he speaks kindly to Joey, bidding him grow up 'strong and straight' for his parents' sake, he is already looking beyond him, into some remote destiny: 'I've got to be going on. A man has to be what he is, Joey. You can't break the mould. I tried it and it didn't work for me. Joey, there's no living with a killing. There's no going back from one. Right or wrong it's the same. The brand sticks.'

Where he is heading we do not know; his direction is governed by symbolism rather than topography. Traditionally the picaresque hero may live through many such adventures, but there is an air of melancholy finality about Shane's departure. His kind of days are over, as the archetype of the hero blends with that of the scapegoat, the man who has assumed the blood guilt which the necessary violence carries.

This hardly squares with Will Wright's conclusion to the 'classical' plot, where since the hero has defeated the villains he gives up his 'special status' and is accepted by the society (1975: 47). In the book something like this occurs, where Shane both preserves his heroic difference ('no bullet can kill that man,' one of the characters insists) while his presence lingers on as a kind of tutelary spirit, inseparable from the Starrett's farm which he has helped to preserve ('he's here, in this place, in this place he gave us,' Marian comforts the distraught Joe). Given the whole conception of the story, it is difficult to see how a more substantial place could be found for him, even if the convention that sees the hero riding off into the unknown were not so strong that in a film like Henry King's *The Gunfighter* (1950) we see Gregory Peck making the customary exit over the final credits, in spite of his funeral in the penultimate sequence.

Perhaps our inquiry has already made it clear that if the western can be discovered in some pure, unmarked form, then Stevens' film is not it. The voice of the genre is inflected in all kinds of ways, many of them contradictory. Although *Shane* reminds us of many of the form's characters and situations, a host of subtle differences robs them of much of their iconic power. Far from fitting Joan Mellen's condemnation as 'an unabashed celebration of the most destructive emblems of maleness in the fifties, the very decade when these values were for the first time subjected to explicit challenge in the American film' (1978: 232), the 'abashed' quality of the picture is its most noticeable feature. In deciding to promote the family to the centre of the story, Stevens inevitably marginalises the hero, who for much of the action is only doing what Joe Starrett can do better. In the novel there is at least some depiction of the inner struggle involved in the hero's attempt to escape his destiny, although the means are often banal, with Shane obliged to take the boy into this confidence for anguished self-communings ('Life's a dirty business, Bob'). Ladd's reserve is certainly more visually impressive, but it leaves too much unsaid. Although Marian's worry over the effect on Shane – insisted on in the book – is retained, in her understanding of the sacrifice he is making in going to meet Wilson ('you were through with gun-fighting'), the obvious social utility of the action called for seems to deprive his punctilio of substance. The 'code' of the westerner, which as Judith Hess Wright says, 'allows for a guiltless existence' (cited in Grant 1986: 44) in justifying violence in clearly defined circumstances, does not seem to be operating for *Shane*, but neither is it explicitly questioned.

In the roughly similar situation in *The Man Who Shot Liberty Valance*, where Tom Doniphon kills the man who would have killed Ranse Stoddard, although Stoddard is his rival for the woman they both love, the means involved – shooting the man from hiding rather than in fair fight – represent a more genuine sacrifice of principle. At a deeper level of course, Ford's film does underwrite Shane's perception: Stoddard is free to thrive because he knows the blood is not on his head, and Tom Doniphon goes into decline at least partly because he has violated his own self-image.

The moral ambiguity of the gunfighter, inevitably raised by the parallels between Shane and Wilson, is deliberately underplayed, although again Palance's vivid characterisation makes Ladd still more bland in comparison. Even the friendship between Starrett and Shane, apparently equally sincere off the set, according to Heflin, potentially a vital element in a genre where strong male friendships are the norm, seems lacking in depth when compared with, say, that between Chance and Dude in Hawks's *Rio Bravo*. Marian's constant presence robs it of any homoerotic overtones and there can be limited give and take when both are strong and self-sufficient characters. The implied sexual rivalry is so thoroughly sublimated that it has little reality, and although it is obviously not true that a love story has no place in a western, if there were no sexual attraction between Shane and Marian, the outcome would presumably be unchanged. Marian makes no real choice; her relationship with Shane is not so very different from that of thousands of safely married women who responded to Alan Ladd on the cinema screen before returning home to cook their husbands' suppers. Similarly, the boy Joey, promoted by the change of medium to a leading actor rather than mere narrative device, really has not enough to do to justify the increased attention. Although in the book we hear of areas of 'adult knowledge beyond my understanding', the limitations of the innocent eye are not caught up into the narrative. Nothing that we see in his presence is in fact too difficult for him to understand, and this is true of the film as a whole with its objective and immediately accessible point of view.

Objections such as these are not a criticism of the histrionic abilities of the performers but of the way in which their roles are conceived, perhaps the result of a mistaken belief that any complexity would obscure the mythic simplicity of their interactions. Depth is not necessarily dependent on ambiguity within individual characters, although that might contribute valuable chiaroscuro. Like the American novel in the nineteenth century, the genre's affinities may be with romance rather than the psychological introspection or social nuance of European fiction in the same period. *Shane* may still strike us as myth only in the weak sense, of being unreal. Whether the complexities derive from historical contingency or more 'universal' moral questions, we need to feel that the action calls them into play, not as problems to be resolved by any final gun-down, but as gains and losses to be cast up in any adequate account of the human condition. The best western films convince us that such a description is not completely out of place, and in the next chapter we shall be looking at three of them.

2   THE ESTABLISHED CLASSICS

Although by the early 1950s the popularity of low-budget westerns and serials was well past its peak, Paramount were nevertheless willing to invest in *Shane* because the genre had acquired a new seriousness, registered by the attention of Bazin and others to the output of directors like Ford, Hawks and Mann. William Pilkington sees Ford's first sound western, *Stagecoach*, as a significant event since it 'rescued the Western from the 'B' movie category and supplied it with a new respectability' (1979: 3). Yet the audience's familiarity with the formula was largely developed through experience of its most banal manifestations, endlessly recycling the basic settings, characters and plots. Indeed, it has often been argued that pre-adolescents' need to satisfy fantasies of power without the complications of adult responsibility explains their appeal. As Cawelti summarises the theory, 'the cowboy hero provides them with an embodiment and justification of the "carefree life" of childhood ... The audience identifies with the hero, who performs violent actions, thereby gratifying the audience's own aggressive wishes, conscious or unconscious' (1971: 9–11). If some elements of this survive in the adult's response to the films, Marlon Brando's embarrassment that his first effort as director, *One-Eyed Jacks* (1961), should result in just another western is perhaps not surprising: 'Will I ever be able to look my friends in the face again?' (cited in French 1974: 5).

Yet while the cowboy hero is partly defined by the formula which places him at the 'intersection between civilisation and the wilderness', in Kitses' terms (1969: 11), and justifies his use of violence in resolving the conflicts that arise, in the work of different film-makers the basic elements take on the colouring of their respective preoccupations. For John Ford the emphasis is on history; the processes through which society comes into being as the garden emerges from the wilderness. In *My Darling Clementine* this is still largely a matter for celebration; later, doubts set in about what is excluded – eventually, in *The Searchers,* the hero himself. The family and the community are at the heart of his vision of America, and Michael Budd's essay 'A Home in the Wilderness' examines its reflection in the visual imagery of the films (Kitses & Rickman 1998: 133–47).

Howard Hawks, as Peter Wollen has noted, also seeks values beyond the individual, in solidarity with others, but 'unlike Ford, he does not give his heroes any historical dimension, any destiny in time' (1969: 82). This is less obviously the case in *Red River*, with its rail head and cattle drives, than in *Rio Bravo,* which is set mainly indoors with little sense of life going on beyond the circle of immediate protagonists. For both Ford and Hawks the forces which threaten the hero and call forth his special skills gener-ally come from outside, what he 'has to do' clearly signalled, but for Mann conflict is usually located within the psyche. If he is, as Kitses argues, char-acteristically a revenge hero, the revenge is often taken upon himself, 'a punishment the inner meaning of which is a denial of reason and humanity' (1969: 33), but itself evidence of a strongly developed moral sense. Simi-larly, whereas in *My Darling Clementine* the 'good' family of the Earps is opposed to the 'bad' family of the Clantons, in Mann's westerns the men the hero has to kill are often friends or relatives. Even the landscape, which acts to enhance the stature of Ford's heroes, to Mann's presents a series of bruising obstacles, while for Hawks there is no backdrop to distract us from the dynamics of the group. The three films that follow should help us to consider these differences in greater depth.

My Darling Clementine

Of all Hollywood directors, Ford is the most closely identified with the western. He got his start in the business with Harry Carey, one of the first stars of the genre, and his contribution lasted about fifty years, down to *Cheyenne Autumn* in 1964. His experience in silent films is clearly visible and he retained a fondness for black and white – 'real photography' as he thought of it – as late *The Man Who Shot Liberty Valance*. Yet in spite of the success of *Stagecoach*, which helped to establish John Wayne as a star, it was another seven years before he returned to the form and the Monument Valley locations for his hundredth film, *My Darling Clementine*.

For the story the screenwriters drew on Stuart Lake's *Wyatt Earp, Frontier Marshal* (1931), although Ford had himself known Earp during his early days in Hollywood and heard his account of the gunfight at the OK Corral. 'We did it exactly the way it had been,' he subsequently claimed (cited in Bogdanovich 1967: 85), but historical accuracy plays little part in *My Darling Clementine*. To quote a famous line from *The Man Who Shot Liberty Valance*, 'when the legend becomes fact, print the legend'. Ford had more use for the already legendary figure of Wyatt Earp than the rather dubious actuality of events in 1881. To play the role he had Henry Fonda, memorable in earlier Ford features, uniquely fitted for the requisite aura of myth, his physical presence so different from that of John Wayne, Ford's other western hero. Wyatt becomes involved when the herd he and his brothers are driving is run off, with the younger brother, who provides a quasi-feminine element to complete the idea of family so important to the director, murdered. A simply material loss, the stolen cattle, would be insufficient justification to confer the moral authority Wyatt must assume. As he later confides over James's grave, he stays on 'so that kids like you can grow up and live safe' – sentiments close to the heart of the film and to those that later motivate Shane's involvement with the Starretts, however archaic they may seem now.

The conflict between the Earps and the Clantons, who soon emerge as the likely culprits, does not have the socio-historical justification of that between the Starretts and Rykers in *Shane* (in reality cattle had nothing to do with it), although the Clantons' lawlessness depends on Tombstone remaining 'wide open'; something the new Marshal is about to change. He is soon in action when a burst of gunfire from a drunken Indian interrupts his shave. The Marshal is unwilling to intervene, so Wyatt takes over;

indeed Wyatt's brutal ejection of him ('Indian, get out of town, and stay out!') has troubled the liberal conscience, even if mitigated somewhat by the basically comic handling of the incident.

Although the Clantons are obvious suspects (we hear they are running cattle) Wyatt seems in no hurry to question them. We find him in the saloon absorbed in a game of poker, although he is, from his chair at the back of the frame, fully aware of what is going on around him. Robert Warshow defined the western hero as essentially 'a figure of repose' (Kitses & Rickman 1998: 36), paradoxically in view of the gunplay which comes with the territory, and this is true of Fonda's watchful, self-contained portrayal.

Watching Wyatt is Chihuahua, Linda Darnell's opulent figure, abundant hair and pouting lips those of a stock figure of the genre. She is signalling the details of his hand to the professional gambler with whom he is playing, eventually prompting him to action, and she finishes up unceremoniously dunked in the horse trough outside. Wyatt's accompanying threat to run her back to the Apache reservation suggests a link with Indian Charlie, and unless we have a taste for robust horseplay raises similar doubts. In fact Chihuahua's gypsyish looks and costume seem Mexican; usually the cinema's sign for sensuality and unreliability. Mexican or Apache, she is, as she tells Wyatt, 'Doc Holliday's girl', preparing us for Victor Mature's impressive entrance soon afterwards.

Those ravaged good looks, frequently in heavy shadow, are the site for the film's most complex oppositions, and without him *My Darling Clementine* would be debilitatingly bland. He is the Easterner who has come west, the healer turned gunman (in real life, less resonantly, Holliday was a dentist), the poetry-reader who runs Tombstone's gambling. In one of the interlocking triangles at the centre of the structure, he has forsaken the WASP Clementine Carter for the seductively 'native' Chihuahua. But potentially he is still Wyatt's rival for Clementine's hand and dominance in Tombstone.

Doc's self-disgust, like Hamlet's, is never really explained, nor is it clear whether his physical ailment (historically accurate – tuberculosis killed him 18 months later) is symbolic of some spiritual malaise, or merely the reason why he runs from Clementine, unwilling maybe to ruin her young life. Holliday, the intellectual of the piece, who has learned of Wyatt's reasons for being Marshal, can articulate them in terms which underline the mythic significance of his role: 'You haven't taken into your head to deliver us from all evil?' We recognise the emergence of the 'Lawman Story', another of Grüber's categories. In accepting the job-description as moral crusader Wyatt again provokes Doc, who has no relish of salvation: 'I see we're in opposite camps'. But when Doc half-seriously draws, he pulls back his coat to show that he is not carrying a gun. This kind of playfulness in place of real conflict could be seen as the 'underlying preoccupation with style' noted by Warshow (1954: 44) and others, a 'softness' marring the film, but one has to admire the skill with which Ford screws up and releases the tension.

Dark shadows are dispelled with the arrival of the actor, that sterling tragedian Granville Thorndyke, bringing culture to the wilderness. Top hat, frock coat and English accent make him an almost Dickensian figure, erupting into the scene with a whirl of farcically swinging doors and animated clichés. In Ford's world the right kind of drinking is always pardonable, and Thorndyke's fondness for the stuff is closer to Doc Boone's in *Stagecoach* than Doc Holliday's solitary self-destructiveness. There seems to be a convention that the more educated elements of the society – doctors, newspaper editors, actors – need to anaesthetise themselves against the rigours of the West.

Here in the saloon, to piano accompaniment, his recitation of Hamlet's most famous soliloquy is oddly moving, to no one more than Doc who leans forward to catch each word, and when the actor breaks down – 'Please help me, sir … it's been so long', takes up Shakespeare's lines himself. He too breaks off in a fit of coughing, at the line 'thus conscience doth make cowards of us all', leaving Wyatt, a sympathetic if uncomprehending witness so far, to dispatch the practical business of getting Thorndyke to the improvised theatre.

A new sequence opens with the arrival of the stage, and with it the film's titular heroine, more than a third into its screen time. Structurally, Clementine's role is clear enough, her modest costume and upright carriage asserting her WASP background in opposition to Chihuahua's more obvious charms in a battle for Doc's soul. But his abbreviation of her name humanises her, and if actions speak louder than words, her pursuit of the man she loves, at some cost to her pride, as she explains to Wyatt, shows that her feelings are as strong as Chihuahua's, if more disciplined. In the later sequence, she can join in the dance, again distinguishing her from, say, Lucy Mallory in *Stagecoach*, part of a slightly similar polarity of Eastern lady and saloon girl. Doc's judgement that 'this is no place for your kind of person' does less than justice to her adaptability, part of the value system the film is moving towards. As it is, she has the authority to judge him: 'You can't run away from yourself'.

Alone in his room, sitting in front of the framed medical diploma, he pours himself a whiskey while contemplating his reflection in the glass. 'Dr John Holliday,' he snarls, before smashing the composite image. Like Oscar Wilde's Dorian Gray, Wyatt moves through the world of experience apparently untouched (in his essay Warshow writes of the western hero's concern for 'the purity of his own image' (1954: 38)) while Doc, like the picture in the attic, succumbs to the ravages produced by the tensions explored in Ford's subsequent films.

If Doc cannot bear to contemplate himself, Wyatt is unable to pass a mirror or window without pausing to check the angle of his hat, and there is something narcissistic in his fascination with his own appearance. More detailed discussion of the ways in which the two characters are 'differently embedded' in the text through the use of mirrors and reflections can be found in Deborah Thomas's recent study, *Reading Hollywood: Spaces and Meanings in American Film* (2001: 14–20). Another bit of physical business seems to symbolise Wyatt's pivotal position in the oppositions which make up the film. A chair is brought out onto the boardwalk, positioned carefully where shade meets the sunlight, and Wyatt proceeds to rock to and fro on its back legs. It is tempting to connect this repeated balancing act with the poise which separates him from the more straightforwardly involved characters like his two brothers, an analogue for the 'moral grace' Lindsay Anderson identifies not too fancifully with the Fonda persona (1981: 14).

The celebrated Sunday morning sequence finds Clementine and Wyatt walking arm in arm along the boardwalk and out of town, to the accompaniment of 'Shall we gather at the river', one of Ford's favourite revivalist hymns. The skeletal wooden tower, with its tolling bell, comes into view, the stars-and-stripes proudly flying, the saguaro cacti in the background and beyond them the familiar sandstone buttes. A dance is to be held on the church floor before the walls and roof are raised.

Clementine is visibly affected by the spirit of the dance, the flowers around her hat also modifying her more prim and proper initial appearance. Wyatt takes longer to thaw out, seemingly constrained by his three-piece suit and the hat which has become almost a running gag. He first removes it then tosses it aside before leading his partner to the dance floor. Opinions are divided on how much of a dancer he is, Fonda's high-kicking style scarcely graceful (although an advance on his clumsy walk with Marjorie Weaver in *Young Mr Lincoln* seven years earlier). This is really the high point of the film, marking his acceptance into the community, a community which finds expression in traditional rituals, here given religious sanction. The mood is sustained as we cut to Sunday lunch at the hotel, Wyatt in the centre of the frame with the carving knife in a scene of domestic harmony and good humour. But Doc's irate entry, angry to find that Clementine has not boarded the midday stage as instructed, strikes a discordant note. Increasingly he figures as a disruptive force, and also here as a reminder that a good deal of the plot has still to unfold although the picture is nearly three quarters over.

Doc is briefly suspected of James's murder but then exonerated when Chihuahua identifies Billy Clanton, although he shoots her to prevent further revelations. Only immediate surgery can save her. In the similar scene in *Stagecoach* Doc Boone had sobered up sufficiently to deliver Mrs Mallory's baby, but Doc Holliday cannot escape his fate; although the operation is successful, the patient dies. Chihuahua, for her part, bravely enduring in soft focus, like the fallen woman of Victorian fiction, finds a kind of purity in death.

At last we arrive at the ostensible subject of the film, the 'clever military manoeuvre' that the ageing Earp had sketched for Ford before his death in 1929 – and which more recent and more realistic versions of the story, like Cosmatos's *Tombstone* and Kasdan's *Wyatt Earp*, have replaced with supposedly more accurate showdowns. It is indicative of Ford's principal concerns that the action sequence should be relegated almost to a coda to the affirmative heart of the picture, the pairing of Wyatt and Clementine. Structurally this resembles *Stagecoach*, which also has two climaxes, the first coming with the successful birth of the Mallory baby and safe arrival of the stage at Lordsburg, the second with the duel which concludes Ringo's feud with the Plummers. The gunfight is a low-keyed affair, filmed almost in silence, involving cautious flanking movements among the wooden fencing of the stockades rather than the lightning draws of more conventional duels. Opportune use of the dust thrown up by the passing stage leaves only Old Man Clanton alive on the one side to mourn his sons, while only Wyatt and Morgan survive on the other. Doc, left exposed by another fit of coughing, is a casualty, although he lasts long enough to dispatch one of the Clantons before collapsing, his white handkerchief fluttering like some Puccini heroine's.

His death, like Chihuahua's, has been cited as evidence of the moral simplifications the film engages in, 'the desire to expunge every trace of moral ambiguity, even the most attractive, from the nascent society' (McBride & Wilmington 1975: 91). It might be truer to say that the logic of Ford's historical thesis involves the extinction of certain kinds of lawlessness, or that Doc raises tragic contradictions which the romantic resolution of the film cannot contain.

One immediate consequence is that it leaves Wyatt's path to Clementine clear, should he choose to take it, although typically Ford subjects the blossoming romance to comic deflation. One of Ford's scriptwriters, Dudley Nichols, saw the director's weakness as his inability to 'create the normal man-woman passions ... I cannot recall one of his films in which the man-woman relationship came off with any feeling or profundity' (cited in Anderson 1981: 241). Apparently it was studio boss Darryl Zanuck who inserted the kiss with which Wyatt and Clementine part in the closing sequence, in place of Ford's intended handshake. However, Ford remembered wanting Wyatt to stay with Clementine, but the studio insisted on dispatching him over the horizon, an interesting testimony to the force of one of the conventions of the genre which sees the hero as an essentially solitary figure. The 'lost and gone forever' lyrics of the title song, heard again at the close, could support this view, but there seems no reason to doubt that Wyatt will return and call in to see Tombstone's new school-teacher, as he promises.

Fonda's Wyatt does seem a stranger to the doubt and inner conflict which destroy Doc Holliday, as perhaps a married man could not be. He never has to make the choice between love and revenge as Ringo does at Dallas's bidding – although there of course the plot intervenes to ensure that he can satisfy both. This same 'untouched' quality is maintained in another function towards the close. Feigning to leave, Clanton goes for a hidden gun, and it is Morgan, not Wyatt, who finally kills him, as though to keep the patriarchal blood off his brother's head. If, as Warshow claims, it is only a moral ambiguity in the hero which 'saves him from absurdity' (in Kitses & Rickman 1998: 39) any such ambiguity has to be located in our response to what, viewed unsympathetically, could be dismissed as 'a simple-minded allegory' (McBride & Wilmington 1975: 90).

The self-consciousness of the film, the leisurely pace, and beautifully composed photography work against any naïve involvement with the characters and plot. *My Darling Clementine* offers itself as an object for contemplation, and Fonda is peculiarly fitted to be both a figure of legend and a distinctively human presence. It is tempting to see Ford's return to the genre both here and in *Wagon Master* (1959) as motivated by the need to find some area that was still the same, where he could be 'assured of certain certainties'. Tempting too to see Fonda's subsequent roles for Ford as charting a slide away from such certainties, a deepening awareness of the human cost they often involve. Yet a good deal of this is implicit in the earlier film, especially if we read back to it from *The Man Who Shot Liberty Valance* which, as has often been noticed, is centred on a similar set of triangular relationships. Here indeed the image of the western hero (we recall Wayne's naïvely idealistic Ringo Kid in *Stagecoach*) is darkened, even violated, as Doniphon shoots Liberty from ambush, before attempting to destroy himself and the home he has been building for Hallie. In contrast, Ranse is a survivor, an Easterner who builds a future which has no room for either Liberty or Tom; while the senator has become famous, Doniphon has become anonymous even in his own town. Ranse marries the girl, though the suggestion is that he never completely supplants her earlier love for Tom, as prickly and uncultivated as the cactus rose he once gave her. Tom, the classical western hero, is a loner; like Ethan Edwards, the role Wayne plays in *The Searchers*, he 'could never really be part of a family', as Ford recognised.

These darker, later pictures constitute the most immediate refutation of hostile accounts of Ford, like David Thomson's assertion that 'the characters are accepted on their own terms ... and never viewed critically', the message 'trite, callous and evasive' (1975: 203–4). Perhaps there is nothing to say to anyone who sees only a 'stupid, beaming farewell' in the closing moments of *Stagecoach*, where Doc and Curly see off Ringo and Dallas, 'saved from the blessings of civilisation', before repairing to the bar. More true to our experience surely is 'a quality altogether more elusive and profound, some kind of moral poetry', the quality the thirty-three-year-old Lindsay Anderson encountered when in the autumn of 1946 at the Odeon, Leicester Square, he first saw *My Darling Clementine* (see Anderson 1981: 14).

The Naked Spur

Contemplating the evolution of the western in the 1950s, André Bazin singled out Anthony Mann as 'the most classical of the young novelistic directors' (1971: 156) and the eleven westerns he made during the 1950s include some striking successes, the five starring James Stewart constituting a partnership second only to that between Ford and Wayne. Eleven years younger than Ford, Mann came to the cinema in the early 1940s after acting and directing in the New York theatre. In describing his work as novelistic Bazin points to more complex psychological detail in the characters and situations than those of stereotypical examples of the form. In *Winchester '73* (1950), the first of the Stewart westerns, the famous rifle serves to focus themes of patricide and fratricide conceivable in any time or place. The opening legend, which informs us that 'an Indian would sell his soul to own one' has little direct bearing on the story to come, but strikes a relevant moral/psychological note, heard again in *The Naked Spur* two years later.

The opening credits are here projected against the snow-topped mountains which often compose the moral terrain of Mann's pictures, forbidding yet challenging, but a sudden downward camera movement takes us to a close-up of a rowelled spur on a rider's boot. Jarring chords in Bronislau Kaper's accompanying score reinforce the image. In talking about 'King Lear', subject of one of his unrealised projects, Mann remembers the moment 'when they jab Gloucester's eyes out with spurs'. In fact we have to wait another 90 minutes for the spur to reappear, first as an improvised crampon enabling the hero to scale the rock face to reach his antagonist, then as a primitive weapon to overcome him. We have already had more startling camera movement and variety of shot than John Ford would tolerate, yet at no cost to the clarity and continuity of the sequence. The first words we hear – 'Don't move. Turn around' – introduce the atmosphere of tension and suspicion rarely to be relaxed in what follows.

Here Howie Kemp, the Stewart character, is tracking down Ben (Robert Ryan) for the reward money he needs to buy back the farm he has signed over to Mary, his faithless fiancée, when he left for the war. Along the trail he is joined by Jesse (Millard Mitchell), an old-timer prospecting for gold, and Roy (Ralph Meeker), dishonourably discharged from the army, though the alliance remains uneasy. The role of bounty hunter is always more problematic than that of the conventional law man, although both might be said to be performing a socially useful task in return for material reward. Later, more cynical, westerns often centred on this figure. Furthermore, in *Winchester '73* the principal anatagonist is the hero's own brother; in *Man of the West* (1958) his virtual stepfather; and in *The Man from Laramie* (1955), although the James Stewart figure is not actually related to the Waggoman family, he precipitates a similar pattern. Even Ben claims old acquaintance, in spite of Howie's protests: 'Quit acting like we was friends'.

Deprived of any moral advantage over the others, Howie has to agree to split the reward money three ways and accept their help to bring in the prisoner. The situation is complicated by the presence of Lina (Janet Leigh), the orphaned girl accompanying Ben, opening up possibilities of sexual

FIGURE 2 *The Naked Spur*

rivalry he is quick to exploit, in addition to probing Howie's strained self-dislike: 'Killing me in self-defence is a lot better than killing me for money. Choosing the way to live, that's the hard part. That's what's eating you, ain't it Howie?' He also plays on Jesse's weakness with his hints of 'a man he knows' who could locate the gold the old man has been looking for all his life. Roy is similarly troublesome, involving the others in a fight with a

hunting party of normally peaceful Blackfoot on account of his earlier attentions to the Chief's daughter. In saving Ben, Howie takes a bullet in the
leg, a literal wound to add to the figurative ones he already suffers. The
sun is still falling through the trees as beautifully as a few moments before
the carnage began, while they mount up to strains of tragic melancholy
on the *cor anglais* and accompanying strings. Howie is the last to leave
the clearing, pausing head bowed to look back over the shadows on the
ground and the spread-eagled body of the Indian he has killed: the cost of
what he has undertaken.

Lina tends his injury while denying that Ben is 'her man' in that sense.
Ben's interest in her is never clearly explained, and as Leigh plays the part,
with her short hair and shining eyes, she is half girl, half woman, not unlike
the Corinne Calvert character, Renee, in *The Far Country* (1954), with her
pigtails and freckled face, whom the James Stewart character, Jeff Webster,
only learns to appreciate when her rival, the more fully sexual Ronda Castle
(Ruth Roman) dies while attempting to save his life. Here too the dialogue
waxes lyrical as he dreamily lists the joys of the settled life: clearing the
land, building on it, bringing in the cattle. Kaper's sensitive score is full
of romantic yearning, hinting at 'Beautiful Dreamer', but turns sour as Lina
flares up in Ben's defence, uncomfortably accurate in judging that however
'mean' he may be, Howie would not have hunted him down if it had not
been for the reward.

Roy, who has been reconnoitring a possible river crossing, returns with
a plan for them to split up, arguing that the injured Howie will make better
time alone. Suspiciously, Howie turns over the paper on which he has
mapped out the rendezvous, and discovers the dishonourable discharge
with its damning character reference. He decides they will stick together,
but viewers may see a link between Roy's piece of paper and Howie's own,
the Wanted notice for Ben with the offered reward deceptively removed.
Once again Mann's characters are interrelated in what can be seen as a
redistribution of aspects of the hero's own personality rather than fully
independent figures. We find neither the 'male bonding' which feminist
critics have attacked in John Ford's westerns nor the 'spontaneous-intuitive
sympathy' which Robin Wood (1968: 52) identifies in Howard Hawks' films.

As Douglas Pye has noted, 'Mann's protagonists are prisoners of a masculinity coded in hopelessly contradictory ways' (Cameron & Pye 1996: 173). The 'professional plot' westerns of Will Wright's structuralist categorisation, including movies such as *The Wild Bunch* (1969) and *Butch Cassidy and the Sundance Kid* (1969), rely on the group to generate the only values which operate meaningfully in the films, but the group in *The Naked Spur* have objectives which bring them into conflict – the reward money, the girl – while the hero's struggle towards true independence seems to be the subject of the film. The fullest expression of the oedipal antagonism in Mann's work comes with *Man of the West* in which Doc Tobin, the monstrous father/villain who rapes his 'son's' woman (Julie London), played right over the top but very powerfully by Lee J. Cobb, is gunned down by Gary Cooper at the film's climax. The reconciliation achieved at the end of *The Searchers* or *Red River* is impossible here.

Nor can the villain be simply relegated to the other side of some moral divide. So far Ben is the only one of the men we have not seen shed blood and his efforts to save his own life seem reasonable enough. Yet before they mounted up we have seen him surreptitiously loosen Howie's saddlegirth; his reminiscences, intercut with shots of the slipping girth, serve as a ruse to put the other man off his guard as they ride along the mountainside, so that when Ben chooses his moment to brush against him, Howie is thrown from his horse and over the edge. In general, the Mann hero suffers and endures whereas the Ford hero – until the darker John Wayne performances in *The Searchers* and *The Man Who Shot Liberty Valance* – has a better time, his problems externalised and no bigger than he can cope with. Howie painfully remounts, watched with concern by Lina, with satisfaction by Ben, who rides forward between the viewer and Howie, as though casting a metaphorical shadow over his endeavours.

When the party take shelter for the night, Ben prompts Lina to take advantage of Howie's growing interest to facilitate his own escape, and they settle down into a two-shot framed by the mouth of the cave. The conversation falters on while she steals glances back at Ben and the strains of 'Beautiful Dreamer' become more distinctly audible. Howie asks what she will do when they get back to Abilene and soon he is telling her about the neighbours he once had and offering her a chance to look at his ranch, when he buys it back – 'With the money you get for Ben?' – but even this cannot interrupt the flow of feeling bringing them together. 'That's something else,' protests Howie, almost whimpering as at last they kiss with the music now welling up on the soundtrack. Immediately we cut away to Ben kicking down the pillar of rock supporting the roof of the cave and heading into the depths.

Howie brings him back to jarring chords, dragging him out of the narrowing tunnel he struggles to enter, a womb-like space if we choose a Freudian reading and see Ben as an alter ego for the hero. There is something regressive about Howie's dream of his ranch, although superficially not so different from Ringo's in *Stagecoach* where he and Dallas will be 'saved from the blessings of civilisation'. But Ringo's points to the future; it is on the other side of the border, the half-built cabin still to be completed. Howie's lies in an almost infantile past which can never be recovered, with the faithless Mary as the betraying female whom the weaned child views with resentment. Yet adult reality has to be faced, and by splitting the masculine role Mann arrives at a statement of some complexity. The shot in which Howie drags Ben back has strong visual echoes of the contrary movement in the earlier sequence where he had dragged himself up towards the saddle on the mountain ridge. We remember Jesse's remark: 'You've got him, but he's got you too'. Perhaps he can free himself by killing Ben, as Roy wishes, before he kills them all. Jesse cuts him loose and sticks a gun in his belt, but as Ben explains, on one of the several occasions where he is allowed the moral upper hand, it would not be a fair fight. Howie's anger and bitterness extend to Lina as she attempts to meet the accusation that she has kept him busy while Ben was making his break. We see her tears, but again a woman has betrayed him.

Defeated this time, Ben next enlists Jesse's help by offering to show him the mine 'his friend' knows of. We understand that Jesse's obsession is not simply a question of materialist greed but, like Howie's desire for his ranch, touched with unreality, and like Howie's his trust will be abused. Once away from the others Ben has no difficulty in overpowering him. Already he has sighted the high rock which provides the ideal vantage point for the ambush he plans. So, with satisfying symmetry, the film circles back to its beginning. Jesse's body will be the bait to halt his pursuers and we cut away to see Howie and Roy mounting up as they hear the shots.

The Naked Spur is the only one of Mann's westerns filmed entirely on location (in the Rocky Mountains of Colorado); we never see a house, only man suffering among awful powers and forms, in Wordsworth's phrase. Now the high rock which we climb with Ben and Lina to the accompaniment of mounting figures in the brass fills the frame, the sound of the raging torrent below increasingly amplified. The scene is set for the final confrontation, the rocky ascent which concludes *Winchester '73*, *The Man from Laramie*, and *Bend of the River* (1952). Jim Kitses sees Mann's cinema as 'pre-eminently a cinema of landscape' and Mann himself said of his heroes that 'the elements make them much greater as actors than if they were in a room. Because they have to shout above the winds, they have to suffer, they have to climb mountains ...' (cited in Kitses 1969: 66).

When Howie and Roy ride up, Lina is able to grab the rifle, spoiling Ben's aim and giving them chance to take cover. Whereas in the opening sequence it was Roy who scaled the cliff, acting incisively while Howie hesitated, as though freed from the moral constraints – or neurotic doubts – which shackle the other, this time Howie will succeed, inching his way up the face, unbuckling a spur to help secure a hold. The only sounds are the roar of the river and the clink of rowel on rock, while in an extraordinary overhead shot with the torrent beneath we see the two men edging towards each other, Ben above and Howie beneath. As Ben stands upright, Howie hurls the spur, catching him in the cheek, and at the same moment Roy, who has been covering his approach, fires repeatedly. As in *My Darling Clementine*, although the hero defeats the villain he does not take his life, the 'unclean' role relegated to Roy, the purely instrumental man. Ben topples into the river but Roy efficiently lassos a tree on the far side and, hanging from the rope, makes for the body. When Lina protests 'Ben's dead – ain't that enough?' Howie pushes her aside, but as he goes to lend a hand, a huge log comes into view. A close-up shows the ugly mass, borne along by the current like some implacable natural force, pushing Roy under in spite of their warning cries. Howie still has the rope attached to Ben and begins to pull him in: 'He's going to pay for my land ... The money, that's all I've ever cared about'. Above the roar of the torrent they must shout to make themselves heard, and not all they say is audible, although the gist is clear enough. Jesse, Roy and Ben are all dead. Howie now has 'no part- ners, like I started'. 'He'll never be dead for you if you take him back,' she counters in desperation as he ties the body across his horse, denying his better self to the last. The terms of the moral debate are familiar enough, but the tension in the dialogue and the power of the physical setting give it a force brilliantly sustained. 'All right, I'll marry you. I'll go with you,' Lina concedes. 'Why? Tell me why,' comes Howie's final attempt, 'I'm going to sell him for money'. Yet the battle is already won, or lost. A close-up of Janet Leigh's face, full of concern, eyes shining with pride against the blue sky, 'Beautiful Dreamer' *fortissimo* this time, as he takes Ben down almost tenderly, a deposition which, in restoring him to his humanity will gain Howie his own.

With Jesse's shovel, Ben can finally be laid to rest, while Lina offers to fix some of Jesse's coffee. There is a parallel with *The Far Country* where the little bell attached to Jeff's saddle, a present from the Walter Brennan character destined for the home he had hoped he and Jeff would one day share, survives him to add its distinctive note to the close of the film. Yet although the camera pans over the enduring mountains to a suitably expan- sive musical theme (again a variant on 'Beautiful Dreamer'), the ending is somewhat muted. In line with the conventions of the genre, Lina figures as the reward for the hero's struggles and the means of reconciling him with society, but she has acted as an obstacle to his immediate desires, and is another responsibility he must assume. In offering herself she deals the final blow to the tottering edifice of his self-sufficiency, and his anguished question 'Why?' expresses more sorrow than joy. 'Do you still want to go to California?' he asks fatalistically, '... that's it, then'. There is no embrace, and the final shot has them riding away from us down the mountain side, littered with the stumps of felled trees, in silence with Jesse's mule beside them as a reminder of what has been lost.

Jim Kitses writes of the 'strangely static quality' of Mann's career (1969: 80), a lack of growth and development that parallels the action of many of the films, and David Thomson (1975) finds a side-stepping of actual issues, a craftsmanship too neatly self-contained. Perhaps these are real limitations – one misses too the humour of Ford or Hawks – but more recently Douglas Pye has argued that the films can be seen as 'male melo-drama' where 'the collapse of fantasy' acquires a positive force (1996: 173). Whether or not one agrees, *The Naked Spur* remains one of the most memo-rable westerns of the 1950s.

Rio Bravo

In a film career almost as long as Ford's, we might not immediately asso-ciate Howard Hawks with the western, yet of his five contributions to the genre between 1948 and 1970, two at least stand out, not because they are especially innovative – on one level, 'his lack of originality is quite stag-gering' (Wood 1968: 11) – but because they accept the conventions of the form while infusing them with peculiarly Hawksian values.

The first of these, *Red River,* would be the top choice for many, a super-western on the epic scale. Russell Harlan's handsome black and white photography makes the most of the six thousand head of cattle hired for the picture, and the moment when he pans to follow them across the tracks while smoke boils from the stack of the halted locomotive is a memorable conjunction of old and new. Montgomery Clift in his first screen role and John Wayne at his most abrasive turn in commanding performances, their oedipal rivalry a means of dramatising the conflicting claims of society and the individual so central to the genre, and to Borden Chase's scripts for Anthony Mann. *Rio Bravo* is very different, intimate rather than epic, as much like *Only Angels Have Wings* (1939) as *Red River*. There was a story, involving the sheriff, played by Wayne, and his heavily outnumbered depu-ties struggling to hold in gaol Joe Burdett (Claude Akins), brother of the local big wheel, until the Marshal arrives to see him tried for murder, but Jules Furthman and Leigh Brackett, long time collaborators with Hawks, used it to generate the characters and situations which, as he said in an interview with Peter Bogdanovich, produced 'almost as many laughs as if we'd started out to make a comedy' (cited in Hillier & Wollen 1996: 64).

FIGURE 3 *Rio Bravo*

It is worth pausing to examine the six-minute opening sequence. A door opens to admit a man (Dean Martin) and, after a brief subjective shot to show the interior of the bar, we pan to follow his hesitant progress along the rear wall to the right. At the bar Joe Burdett looks up, recognising with amusement the drink he is pouring as the focus of the other's attention. Wordlessly the fact is acknowledged and a coin produced. So far the soundtrack has consisted of the buzz of conversation and a desultory Spanish guitar; now, as the coin is thrown, Dimitri Tiomkin's score underlines the clink of the dollar as it hits the spittoon which a sudden close-up reveals at Dean Martin's feet. Tension subsides again as the camera moves down to follow him as he stoops slowly to retrieve it, but then the spittoon is kicked violently away and we cut to a low-angle shot of John Wayne towering disapprovingly, almost as impressive an entrance as his first appearance in *Stagecoach* twenty years before. As he turns away, Martin seizes a length of wood and strikes him to the floor. When the man at the bar laughs he goes for him too, but is forcibly restrained. In a reversal of the basically rightwards direction of the sequence, Burdett steps away from the bar and with calculated cruelty begins to beat him up, blows to the stomach punctuated in the musical score. When another man lays a restraining hand on his arm, in close-up we see a gun drawn and fired at point blank range. Hawks is as sparing with the close-up as Ford, and here the effect is not dramatic excitement – the action is quite unhurried and the musical accompaniment ignores it – but logical demonstration, the victim registering surprise rather than pain. The villain reveals the moral blankness and contempt for life against which the heroes must assert themselves. He swaggers from the bar and out along the street, manhandling a Mexican woman on the way in case we should still be in doubt about his villainy. We go with him through the swing doors of another bar where he signals for a drink, his back towards us as, like us, he hears the thud of a door swing shut and turns to see Wayne advancing unsteadily, forehead bloodied and a rifle in his right hand: 'Joe, you're under arrest'. These are the first words we hear, but Wayne seems likely to be defeated when one of the men behind him draws: 'Now what are you going to do, sheriff?' A cut shows us that Martin has come in too, and he steps forward adroitly to take another man's gun from its holster and shoot to disarm the man covering Wayne: 'You can do just about what you want, Chance.' Continuing the alternation of relative stasis and violent action which characterises these initial sequences, Chance whirls to lay out Joe with a single blow from the barrel of his rifle, and Martin gives him a hand to drag the body out through the doors at the back of the frame. A muffled drum accompanies the movement, and proves to be an overlap for the next scene, where it leads a funeral procession towards the camera. Already, with a minimum of dialogue, the action unfolding in actual time so the effect is almost that of a single long take, we have been given the basic structure of the narrative: the fall and rise of the Dean Martin character, the drunk who regains his self-respect.

The rest of the cast assemble: Pat Wheeler (Ward Bond), an old acquaintance of Chance's, and his new man Colorado (Ricky Nelson), bringing a wagonload of dynamite into the already explosive situation. The weight of the picture is distributed fairly evenly among the players, the all-male group to be completed with the addition of Stumpy, the fellow with the shotgun guarding the gaol (Walter Brennan, minus his top teeth, embellishing with comic gusto a stock figure of the genre, the sidekick who serves to demonstrate that the hero is capable of affection and even tenderness). How well they will 'do' is the question for the rest of the film.

At the hotel we meet Carlos and his wife Consuela, adding ethnic colour and comedy, but as Wood (1968) argues, also a courage and dignity which transcends their origins in the stock type of the excitable Mexican. The female interest, Feathers (Angie Dickinson), a variant of the 'good bad girl' very different from Claire Trevor's Dallas in *Stagecoach*, although both fall for John Wayne, functions initially as a challenge to Chance's authority but is soon doing her bit to help out. It is well known that Hawks and Wayne undertook *Rio Bravo* partly in reaction to *High Noon*, in which small-town America leaves the Marshal to face the villains alone. Here there is no shortage of assistence, though Colorado is only enlisted after his boss Wheeler is shot by one of Burdett's men.

The stage is set for one of those tests of physical courage and mutual trust around which Hawks's action dramas so often revolve. Self-deprecating irony undercuts the heroics. Recently Dude has debarred the front door of the saloon where the killer has taken refuge; now he would like to try it while Chance takes the back: 'Think you're good enough?' 'I'd like to find out.' 'So would I.' Since Wheeler's killer ran through a puddle, he should have mud on his boots; Dude's task is to identify him, but as the men line up and no trace of mud appears, the situation begins to slip away. Laughter is followed by another coin in the spittoon. A brief overhead shot has already shown us the killer on the balcony but now, at the critical moment, when even an admonitory stare from Chance may not be enough to keep Dude up to the mark, a close-up reveals a glass of beer on the bar at his elbow. Blood drips down the side, and feinting to accept the offered drink, he takes a few paces forward, wheels, kneels and fires in a single movement, to bring the killer crashing to the floor. In retrospect we see that although Dude's skill and nerve have been vindicated, there is an element of pure chance in the happy outcome. Hawks' view of the universe includes a stoical recognition that even courage and comradeship might not be enough. Yet it is the best we have.

After the excitement of the previous sequence, the film enters on a more leisurely phase, picking up the threads of the various relationships in line with Hawks' preferred method, 'an elaboration of the characters rather than the articulation of a plot' (Hillier & Wollen 1996: 65). Colorado hands over Wheeler's possessions to Chance, and Dude wonders if he is as good as Wheeler said, prompting one of those home-spun aphorisms so dear to the genre: 'I'd say he was so good he doesn't feel he has to prove it'. At the hotel, Feathers apologises to Chance for having 'got out of line' by taunting him at their previous encounter, unaware of the pressure he was under. It is tempting to see John T. Chance's name as suggesting his function, that of giving others a chance to fulfil themselves.

There is nothing approaching the populist stance of Shane and Starrett on behalf of the little man against the wealthy landowners. Society is, of course, threatened by the villains, but the man Joe killed remains anonymous. Chance is just doing his job, rather than setting out to deliver us from all evil. Morality is less an overt social construct than, in Hemingway's phrase, 'what makes you feel disgusted afterwards'. Friendship and professional respect are the basis for conduct, with 'society' in the larger sense as absent as in *The Naked Spur*.

The absence of a positive social ideal has been noted in many films of the late 1950s, a condition for the development of 'the professional plot' in Will Wright's formulation, where the heroes generate their own shared values. John Lenihan finds a parallel with contemporary indictments of the 'placid and conformist' (1980: 115) character of post-war America in a series of films, *High Noon* among them. *Rio Bravo* may seem to fit the pattern, but we must remember its similarity to *Only Angels Have Wings* (1939) 20 years earlier when looking for any simple reflective model.

Back at the gaol, Chance joins Stumpy and Dude, and Colorado comes over to explain that the music which for some time has been issuing from the Burdetts' saloon is the *deguello*, the tune the Mexicans played at the Alamo in 1836; the cut-throat song meaning 'no quarter'. Chance rolls a cigarette, and when Dude's attempts to do the same are frustrated by his fumbling fingers, hands it to him. In interview Hawks commented on the way in rehearsal they would take a piece of business like this 'to start some relationship going and then further it'. The time seems right to hand over Dude's guns, which – unknown to him – Chance had recovered from the man he sold them to when desperate for drink, in one of the little touches which, together with the perfectly judged playing, makes the scene so affecting but so hard to summarise.

Dude's rehabilitation is not yet complete and the next development of the plot finds him overpowered by Burdett's men, and only the intervention of Colorado and Feathers allowing Chance to keep his prisoner in gaol. Sunk in self-pity, Dude painfully registers his own exclusion as the younger man is sworn in as deputy. 'Is he as good as I used to be?' his inquiry elicits one of the film's memorable lines: 'It'd be pretty close. I'd hate to have to live on the difference.' 'Then you got the best of it. Him for me.' Dude unpins his star and with shaking hands reaches for the bottle. Chance tactfully looks away as Dude raises the glass, at once concealing and signalling how much hangs on the decision. Suddenly the strains of the Alamo music start up again and Stumpy goes to shut the window. 'Stumpy, don't close it'. Dude straightens and pours the contents of his glass back into the bottle, without spilling a drop. It is one of the great moments in the genre's history, strong enough to carry the overt message – 'Until they played that piece I'd forgotten how I got into this thing. If they keep on playing it, I don't think I'll ever forget again'. It shows that this is not only Dean Martin's story in terms of the plot but because he gives a performance in no way overshadowed by Wayne's compelling presence. It is true that this is the turning point of the film, although there are more obstacles in store and Dude will be captured again, this time through no fault of his own.

The song sequence which follows it might be dismissed as a mere concession to the fact that the cast includes two recognised singers, but Robin Wood is surely right to draw attention to the contribution it makes to the 'spontaneous-intuitive sympathy' on which so much of the picture depends (1968: 52). The fade-in on Martin, fully relaxed for the first time, hat tipped forward over his eyes, feet in the air, is highly expressive as he sings of his 'three good companions – my rifle, pony, and me'. His companions here, Stumpy and Colorado, join in on mouth organ and guitar, potential rivalry between Dude and the younger man forgotten in newly established harmony, though the rich dark sonorities of Martin's voice establish his authority over Nelson's more straightforward delivery. In making music together they generate a communal feeling in direct opposition to the menace of the *deguello*. Chance does not join them and Wood not too fancifully suggests that he is excluded from the charmed circle (although he clearly enjoys what he hears) by his very infallibility. The more fallible mortals – Dude, Stumpy, and Colorado – share a humanity from which the mythic hero is always a little apart.

But all play their part the next morning when, at the creek by the Burdetts' warehouse Dude, again in their hands, is to be exchanged for Nathan's brother. Tiomkin's unobtrusive musical score builds towards the ritual tension of the final confrontation. Wood claims further that unlike *Red River*, *Rio Bravo* has not a single shot that is visually beautiful, but he might have made an exception for the one which frames Chance in the doorway, the sides of the screen blacked out as he steps away from us into the sunlight. The prisoners are turned loose, as agreed, and set to walk towards each other, but when they draw level Dude hurls himself at Joe and bundles him into the shelter of a projecting wall while Chance and Colorado blaze away. Dynamite from Wheeler's wagons comes into play, as we move from the 'real' world to the shooting gallery where the emphasis is on carnival rather than carnage, whatever the implied body count. Perhaps we can justify the scene as a celebration of joyous release after the tension of the previous two hours, but probably no one ever wished it longer, and indeed once Burdett's men surrender we return to the darkness of the town for the film's closing moments.

Dude and Colorado patrol the street, whistling in harmony, stride matching stride, on their way to the gaol for the final reunion. At the hotel, Chance finds Feathers donning the minimal costume she proposes to wear for her song and dance number down in the bar. It might be seen as a weakness of the film that the romance plot and the rehabilitation theme do not sufficiently converge (Stumpy and Feathers never meet), but Chance's role underpins both. He can now give Feathers his full attention, although they find their way towards each other through comic disagreements. Peter Wollen notes that the women in Hawks' films gain admission to the male group only after a long ritual courtship, and even then are never fully accepted (Wollen 1969). Certainly Feathers is not auditioning for the conventional role of wife and mother, nor that of honorary man, a 'pal' who can join in with the boys. Her hourglass figure, echoed in the curves of the screen behind which she changes, is irreducibly feminine, and Chance must accept her as she is, acknowledging her life before she met him, and he does it in his own characteristic way: 'you wear those things in public and I'll arrest you'. Although he has not said he loves her, as they both recognise, 'it means the same thing'. His objection to the revealing tights was that he did not want anyone but him to see her wear them, and he turns to toss them out of the window.

In the street below they fall at the feet of Stumpy and Dude, out taking the air. Stumpy's appreciative cackle blends with Martin's offscreen rendering of the title song as the two men walk away from us into the darkness. Good-humoured to the last, *Rio Bravo* could perhaps seem superficial, but when attempting a summary like that above one realises how detailed it is, although without the more explicit dramatic effects of Ford or Mann. As has often been said, the camera seems simply to have been set up in the most natural position to clarify the action, the *mise-en-scène* is always engaging and informative, the colours rich but muted, the script and acting witty yet moving; the physical impact of Hawks' picture says it all.

Hawks's subsequent westerns, *El Dorado* (1966) and *Rio Lobo* (1970), both starring Wayne, show little further development, as Wood concedes, although he wants to argue that Hawks at his best is '*both* progressive and conservative' [emphasis in original] (Kitses & Rickman 1998: 194). In the next chapter we shall consider what kind of changes are possible within the form.

3　DEVELOPMENT AND CHANGE: THREE FILMS ABOUT JESSE JAMES

It is tempting to see changes within the body of work of the great auteurs in terms of personal development, so that different treatments of Wyatt Earp and the Indian in *My Darling Clementine* and *Cheyenne Autumn*, eighteen years later, become a matter of Ford's disillusion and desire to make amends. Yet clearly changes in society and the cinema audience between the 1940s and the 1960s were a determining factor in what found its way onto the screen. Some of these changes can be illustrated in the modification of the outlaw hero, a regular figure of the genre from the earliest days. Jesse and his brother Frank first appeared in *The James Boys in Missouri* (1908) after numerous printed accounts of their adventures, but Fox's big-budget 1939 Technicolor version, *Jesse James*, consolidated their fame and focused on the attempted bank raid at Northfield Minnnesota in 1876 as the turning point of their fortunes.

The director, Henry King, apparently visited the James farm in Missouri while working on the film, but Jon Tuska is probably right when he describes it as 'a pastoral fantasy, totally misrepresenting all of the major issues and personalities' (1985: 141). As the film ends the Major, standing at Jesse's grave, speculates on some of the elements that feed this fantasy: 'Maybe it's because he was bold and lawless, like we all of us like to be sometimes. Maybe it's because we understand a little that he wasn't altogether to blame for what his times made him ... or maybe it's because he was so good at what he was doing'. The appeal, then, is as old as Robin Hood, and the familiar 'Ballad of Jesse James' even has him robbing the rich to give to the poor, but more immediately the outlaw represents an extreme instance of the individualism that is central to the myth of the West. The hero is 'outside of society', in Wright's formulation (1975: 142), the frontier where we so often find him, a boundary beyond which the law scarcely operates. The fallibility of the law explains why, as we saw in *Shane*, the community needs the hero, even while not fully accepting him, his lifestyle a challenge to its own more settled ways, and in some respects not sharply distinguished from that of the villains.

The outlaw hero is poised between the wilderness and civilisation, self-interest and social responsibility. Ford's Ringo 'used to be a good cowhand, but – things happen' and he finds himself outside the law, and while retaining that essential goodness, freed from the restraints which inhibit the law's pursuit of natural justice. King's film dates from the same year as *Stagecoach* and Fenin & Everson (1977) record a spate of sanitised outlaws in the films of the early 1940s, including Fox's sequel *The Return of Frank James* (1940), part of a 'tremendous upsurge' in historical westerns generally, where the protagonists are scarcely distinguishable from more straightforwardly swashbuckling heroes like Errol Flynn in Michael Curtiz's *Dodge City* (1939). In the following decade, loveable rogues give way to more troubled figures, as indicated by the casting of that other colourful standby of the outlaw picture, Billy the Kid (1859–81). A trawl through films dating back to 1911 shows him impersonated by Roy Rogers, Bob Steele, Buster Crabbe, Audie Murphy, Paul Newman, Michael J. Pollard, and Kris Kristofferson, among others. In *The Left-Handed Gun* (1958), Paul Newman's Billy is a disturbed adolescent, and there is a shift of emphasis from action to psychology which Jonathan Bignell in 'Method Westerns' (in Cameron & Pye 1996) connects with similar developments in other genres, most memorably Nicholas Ray's *Rebel Without a Cause* (1955). However, the stress on the actor's performance does not contradict Lenihan's point that increasingly 'the problem of personal reconciliation with society related directly to, or accompanied failings within, the society itself' (1985: 115).

However, the notion that the determining factor is not the society depicted in the films but 'the attitudes, beliefs, concerns, and deepest desires of the era (for convenience, read *decade*) in which they were made' (Pilkington & Graham 1979: 10) has come under vigorous attack from Jon Tuska, who finds it 'totally spurious' (1985: 8). However, even if he is right that westerns do not so much explore a historical situation, past or present, as 'dream it up', the nature of the dream changes over time. Indeed, even when the film is made, its meaning changes for subsequent generations of viewers, as is persuasively demonstrated in Bob Baker's '*Shane* through Five Decades' (Cameron & Pye 1996).

To return to 1939 and *Jesse James*, it is hard to believe that the Depression does not count for something in the original conception and reception of the film. There are clear similarities between the situation here and that at the start of *The Grapes of Wrath* (1940), where the following year producer Darryl Zanuck and scriptwriter Nunnally Johnson collaborated and again cast Darwell and Fonda as mother and son. The plight of the Oakies in Steinbeck's novel may have inspired the treatment here, since the real-life Jesse's move into crime is less clearly motivated.

Jesse James

'After the tragic war between the states,' begins the legend following the titles set to a heroic march theme, 'America turned to the winning of the west'. This is the last we hear of the Civil War which played a large part in shaping the careers of the James brothers, who fought on the Confederate side. On this occasion at least, the popular cinema seems anxious to leave such contentious issues for simpler moral oppositions.

The unscrupulous railway men are intimidating farmers into selling their land, but the James family hold out, Frank (Henry Fonda) and Jesse (Tyrone Power) coming to the aid of their mother (Jane Darwell). Barshee, the rail agent, comes across as a city slicker invading the rural scene. In the fight that follows he is worsted, but a close-up of a scythe hanging in a tree leads to a final vicious attack, defeated only when Jesse shoots him in the hand. His mother is helped into the house while Pinkie, the faithful black retainer, is dispatched for a doctor and to summon the local farmers to a meeting.

We cut to the prominently signed offices of the 'Liberty Weekly Gazette', where the editor is dictating a leader on the swindling railroads to his niece Zee (Helen Kelly). With his colourful language and abundant 'cuss-words', Uncle Rufe, or 'The Major' as he is generally known, is in a well-established cinematic tradition of battling newspaper editors. Henry Hull plays the part for comedy, the formulaic nature of his invective a running gag. Events then take on a darker tone, as after Frank and Jesse are persuaded to go into hiding a raid on the farm leaves their mother dead.

The sequence has some historical foundation in an incident in 1875, but only after the James gang had been robbing trains for several years. The Pinkertons were enlisted to capture them and an explosion killed Jesse's nine-year-old half-brother and led to the amputation of his mother's arm. The element of the grotesque in this might have appealed to later film-makers, but Henry King has more use for a martyr's death.

Zee's efforts cannot deflect her lover from his perceived duty ('I can't help it Zee, I've just got to'); Barshee is killed in a fair fight but from now on Jesse has a price on his head and his career as a train robber is under way. He dons the bandanna mask of the western outlaw, and in one of the most spectacular moments in the picture, makes his way forward along the carriage roofs in silhouette above the lighted windows below. It is to become a cliché of the genre, and in *The Missouri Breaks* (1976) Jack Nicholson executes the same manoeuvre, as though aware that this is what train robbers are supposed to do, but wishing there were some less dangerous way of earning a living.

The local Marshal, played by Randolph Scott, emerges as Jesse's rival for Zee, although sympathetic to the provocation he has endured and unmoved by the threats of McCoy (Donald Meek), the president of the railway company. The grasping railroads – dispossessors of the honest poor – emerge as the villains leaving law and order, as embodied by

Will, free to join Jesse in shared esteem for love, in the person of Zee, and justice.

She begs him to accept the offered amnesty ('it'll get in your blood, you'll get like a wolf, just doing it because it's your nature') and he agrees, if she will marry him first. The historical Jesse married his cousin Zerelda Mimms in 1874 but not as part of any such deal. We dissolve from their embrace to the two of them in wedding finery, driving through the sun-dappled forest to a white wooden church with Frank and half a dozen others in attendance. 'And then the prodigal son came home to his Ma and Pa,' are the preacher's words as we go inside to join the congregation. Nearby, Will is waiting for Jesse to hand over his guns and accompany him into town. Judge Matthews means to go as light as the law allows, but they have not allowed for McCoy, and the sequence ends with Jesse clutching the bars as the cell door closes. Although he escapes, in a sequence filmed in conventional but exciting parallel montage which ends when they scatter handfuls of banknotes to distract and delay their pursuers, from now on a montage of hotel registrations under false names and temporary rented rooms suggests the best he and Zee can hope for (in one of them we see the sampler she has been working on: 'God Bless Our Home'). After the birth of their son, Zee moves back to the Major's, where the Marshal is increasingly attentive and Jesse magnanimously decides it is best to leave them in peace.

Five years pass, and in Liberty a caller appears with an advert for the Major's paper. A suspiciously affable fellow, he introduces himself as Remington, chucking young Jesse under the chin as he brings news of a state amnesty for any gang member who will kill Jesse, and a new sequence has Remington calling on a woman in a poke bonnet, hoeing in the garden of her shack. She admits she is Mrs Bob Ford but denies having seen her husband recently, although we see him hiding at the window. John Carradine, the fastidious Southern gambler of *Stagecoach*, plays him as a melodramatically obvious villain as he reads details of a possible rendezvous on the back of Remington's card. We join the other members of the gang at their hideout, Jesse's moral decline signalled by a five o'clock shadow and rumpled clothes. Tom expresses their 'respect' for him and his 'troubles', but they cannot share his suicidal recklessness. Tyrone Power conveys his anger by knocking over a chair and frowning a lot, before slapping Tom's face and ordering them all outside. Frank returns to give his brother the heart to heart talk he obviously needs. Jesse is still man enough to recognise the moral force of Frank's reprimand: 'Somebody had to tell you before it was too late'. He apologises and Frank goes out to bring the others back, while Bob Ford makes a shifty entrance. Close-ups of Jesse's unsuspecting back and Bob's pop-eyed mixture of greed and fear show us what he has in mind, but he has not the courage to take the opportunity before the others file in for reconciling handshakes and final arrangements for the proposed raid on Northfield.

We dissolve to the gang riding in over a bridge in the long dusters that are to become part of the iconography of the Northfield raid, to dismount outside the bank. Bob Ford has betrayed them and when the shooting starts we are encouraged to see them as victims rather than aggressors, and although Jesse is hit in the shoulder they fight their way out without killing any of the locals. Finding the ends of the street blocked, they escape by jumping their horses spectacularly through the glass of a shop window. We cut to the Major reading the newspaper report of the raid to Will and Zee. Will tells her he is no longer the Jesse she knew and loved: 'He ain't a knight any more, fighting the bad railroad. He's a wild animal. You can't love him, nobody can.' A lap dissolve shows Jesse arriving by night at their old house, concealed in a farm cart, and dragging himself upstairs, ragged and exhausted. The door opens, letting in the morning light and Zee, who hurries to his bedside: 'My poor hurt darling,' she cries, making one realise how good Claire Trevor and Louise Platt were in *Stagecoach*, or how much better directed.

Another newspaper headline tells us that three months have passed, with no sign of the brothers. We see Jesse and Zee planning their departure for California when Pinkie announces two gentlemen: Bob Howard and his brother Charlie. They claim to have news from Frank, with plans for another raid. Jesse seems to be about to succumb when he hears his son's voice from outside the window: 'Daddy, daddy, I want to come in'. His mind made up, he bids the Howards goodbye and shows them to the door. Temptation safely overcome, Zee and Jesse laugh and sing as she prepares to pack the family Bible, while he gets up on a chair to take down 'God Bless Our Home'. We know the rest. Ominously the camera lingers on Jesse's back as the door opens, and Bob reappears, with shaking hand raising his gun.

To stately music the Major delivers the funeral oration before unveiling the gravestone with Jesse's dates and the information that he was 'murdered by a traitor and a coward whose name is not worthy to appear here'. His tribute nicely sums up the film's conflicting attitudes to the hero: 'There ain't no question about it. Jesse was an outlaw ... Even those that loved him ain't got no answer to that. But we ain't ashamed of him. I don't know why – I don't think even America is ashamed of Jesse James'. The music wells up and Jesse takes his place in the pantheon along with Abe Lincoln, Davy Crockett and the rest. 'All I do know is he was one of the doggonedest, golddingdest, deadblamedest buckaroos that ever rode across these United States of America.'

The Great Northfield Minnesota Raid

Uncle Rufe's pieties claim to speak for all of us, whatever the humorous possibilities of their overemphasis, but the hyperbole of the voice-over behind Philip Kaufman's title sequence is addressed to a more knowing and cynical age: 'In all the world they were the greatest outlaws, they were the greatest revolver fighters, the greatest train, stagecoach and bank robbers that ever lived'. As the gang gallop towards us in close formation to the strains of hoe-down guitar and harmonica, the freeze-frames of individual members are picked out in close-up: 'Frank James was there, armed with his Navy Colt and Bible ... and Bob Younger, the youngest Younger.' Typical of Kaufman's deconstructionist approach is the relegation of Jesse to a supporting role, with top billing going to Cliff Robertson as the true hero of the film: 'And of course Jesse James was there, riding side by side with the great Cole Younger.' The explanatory montage that follows is along familiar lines, a map of Missouri yielding

FIGURE 4 *The Great Northfield Minnesota Raid*

to racing locomotive wheels, claims being staked, monochrome footage of dispossessed farmers as the voice-over intones a comically simplified version of the aftermath of the Civil War: 'Everywhere men from the railroads were driving poor defenceless families from their homes.' The grainy, 'authentic', shots of Clay County and its inhabitants are accompanied by exaggerated sound effects as 'the fresh wind' announced in the commentary begins to blow and 'the James and Younger boys' burst through the screen 'coming to the rescue'. 'From that moment onward they were outlaws, but the people of Missoura would never forget what the boys had done for them.'

Here their antagonist is 'the greatest detective of them all, Allan Pinkerton', hired by the railroads and determined to catch up with the outlaws before the proposed amnesty comes into effect. His three-piece suit with watch-chain prominently displayed is that of the city slicker as he takes up the dialogue to urge his men in pursuit. And so, when the voice-over signs off with the promise of 'the *true* story of the Northfield raid' it is signalling its own rhetoric, rather than advancing a serious claim to belief.

Our first view of the James brothers is in marked contrast to their introduction in King's 1939 version where we find them occupied in honest toil about the house and fields. Here the buzzing of a fly announces their concentration on more basic bodily functions, side-by-side in the john. The paper they use has been left there by Cole Younger, with plans of raids no longer to be executed now that the amnesty has been offered. Outside, Cole is regaling an admiring crowd of children and old men with his tall stories of the 'wonderments' he has seen. He opens his shirt to reveal the quarter-inch leather vest he wears, with its fourteen bullet holes, although – as he admits – 'It ain't hard to get shot. It's the getting back up'. Already we see something of the combination of imaginative freedom and practical realism on which Kaufman bases the character, a foil for Jesse's psychopathic delusions and low cunning.

Cole's 'visionary' powers are revealed when he is ambushed by Pinkerton's men at the local whorehouse, where he is evidently a familiar figure – his enthusiasm for sex is presented as one of his engaging features – distorted images of girls with Scandinavian features and other details pre-echoing later sequences in the film overlap on the soundtrack with the mumblings of the Granny Woman, enlisted by another member of the gang, Charlie Pitts (Wayne Sutherlin), to tend Cole's wounds. Charlie, 'the Ozark medicine man' of the titles, with his long hair and silver earring, owes more to the counterculture of the 1960s than the actualities of Missouri in the 1870s. Frank, at the bedside clutching his Bible, suggests a prayer, with Henry Fonda's shining rectitude reduced to sanctimonious sycophancy in John Pearce's reinterpretation of the role. Jesse proposes a retaliatory raid behind enemy lines, rousing the gang to near hysteria with his bizarre pulpit oratory and staring eyes, as he announces their objective, vouchsafed to him in a vision: the bank at Northfield. Whooping wildly as the music surges up on the soundtrack, they gallop out of the cave and head north. En route they call on Clell Miller (R. G. Armstrong), a former gang member, at his mule farm, although his stiff-backed wife is against the idea of his joining them.

With over 400 miles to go the Youngers decide to take the train. Cole is soon in conversation with a fellow passenger who shares his interest in 'the marvels of mechanics', but he also has news from the State Legislature, a flashback accompanied by his voice-over taking us to a behind-the-scenes deal in which Pinkerton pays off the speaker to rule the decision of the amnesty board out of order. We recognise a recurrent function of the outlaw story: the heroes are driven to go outside the law only when the representatives of the law deny them justice.

They enter Northfield, wearing the essential iconographic long dusters which are part of their disguise as cattle-buyers. Northfield is a large town, as indeed by 1876 it was, with factories and colleges, and as they dismount a team of baseball players walk past. A few moments later the simple Clay County boys back away in alarm from a traction engine, clanking and puffing down the street on its way to the timber yard (a sly allusion perhaps to the similar engine in King's film, as the alias Cole adopts – 'Mr King' – may be). Across the street we see the First National bank, but Cole is drawn rather to the steam calliope set up outside. Inside the office, he has a proposal for Wilcox (Robert H. Harris), the manager: 'You drive a shrewd bargain,' he chuckles, 'but why not? Everybody's doing it, from Jay Gould and Jim Fisk, right on up to President U. S. Grant himself.' Needless to say, the scheme – which involves persuading the citizens to deposit enough money in the bank to make it worth robbing – has no historical foundation, but Wilcox's speculative mania reflects the chicanery of the Gilded Age accurately enough. The comedy is heightened with the arrival of the bank-guard to accompany the loaded bag of gold Cole will use as a decoy; he is played by Elisha Cook Jr., the most put-upon of western bit-players since his abortive duel with Jack Palance in *Shane*.

After a brief return to Pinkerton and his men on the train, now heading north to pick up the trail, we rejoin the rest of the gang as they reach Minnesota and encounter an old widow about to be evicted from her home by the rapacious landlord. The incident, with Jesse providing the necessary eighty dollars and then holding up the landlord to get it back, recurs in several accounts as part of the mythology surrounding the benevolent view of the gang's activities, but Kaufman blackens the comedy. The American family and its values, at the heart of King's film, are replaced by weird distortions – as in many horror films of the early 1970s – when she talks of her 'children', in fact the collection of dolls she keeps in a trunk. Jesse 'adopts' one of them, a miniature Uncle Sam with stars-and-stripes costume, which he then sells to the landlord as they stop him, riding through the wood. After introducing himself and the others, Jesse shoots the man in cold blood. When Bob suggests that they should at least remove the doll, in case it incriminates the old woman, Jesse answers: 'Well, she's a Yankee too.'

When the Jameses and Youngers are at last reunited in Northfield, communal hilarity continues in the local bathhouse, but diametrically opposed views of the forthcoming raid emerge. Jesse proposes to blow the town to kingdom come: 'This ain't a business contraction Cole, it's a guerilla raid. We ain't in it for the money.' Cole sees no need for violence; he will simply make a 'withdrawal' from his partner Wilcox, and the money will go to buy back an amnesty. In the meantime he proposes to treat them to a celebration at 'a little place of light love', though Jesse shows no enthusiasm for the idea. We cut to the brothel where Silent Jim and one of the girls revolve in a slow waltz to a melancholy Scandinavian song. The mood swings between sadness and contentment. Cole explains to Kate his love for 'wonderments ... something to behold, something rare, something good,' which might be a beautiful feeling, or a picture, or an example of the mechanical inventiveness of the coming age, like the telephone. The hand-held camera follows him unsteadily along the passage with several women clinging to him, into the bedroom where we assume he performs prodigious feats. Outside, thunder rumbles as the men emerge in silence through sheets drying on the line to join Frank, Jesse, and Chadwell who have been waiting for them to finish. The storm breaks before they reach town, and rain is falling on the abandoned calliope as they dismount in front of the bank. Dave Grusin's music, for most of the film guitar-based ethnic folk, adds a harpsichord and wood block for more sinister overtones. As we know, the raid fails, although here Cole's fascination with the dysfunctional calliope unleashes a deafening discord which raises the alarm. The mixture of comedy and violence is maintained as the survivors head for the doll-woman's house, where they find a warm welcome. She is, Jesse claims, 'like a second mother'. Bob's injuries are explained as the result of 'just a fight over some money'. 'Ain't that always the way,' she clucks sympathetically. We cut to the dispirited posse about to give up the hunt before returning to the doll woman, setting out to get a doctor she can trust. Jesse and Frank accompany her, and we see them shepherding her away, under a sheltering umbrella.

Somewhere else in the forest the posse come across the murdered landlord and the doll Jesse had left behind, which with a nice irony will lead them to their quarry. The camera repeats the circling movement of the brothel scene, this time to show the interior of the doll-woman's house with the exhausted outlaws trying to rest. Charlie wakes, and we see a flashback of the granny woman and her warning before unseen guns begin to blast away, shattering the windows and ornaments and causing Cole to writhe where he sits (echoes perhaps of the bloody finale of *Bonnie and Clyde*) as the bullets tear into his chest. As silence falls over the room, we cut to a perky guitar-picking theme and a buggy crossing a field, driven by Frank with Jesse at his side, holding the widow's basket and umbrella and now wearing her clothes. 'Better cover up them bloodstains,' Frank advises, as Robert Duvall adds transvestism to his other oddities. He is already planning to get together a new gang: 'What's that good-looking kid's name? Bob Ford? I think he'd fit in just right.' The joke depends on our knowledge that Bob Ford was, in the words of the ballad, 'the dirty little coward' who, some six years later, 'laid Jesse James in his grave'.

At last Pinkerton and the train reach Northfield, to find a band playing and the posse returning, triumphantly accompanying the battered survivors from the doll-woman's house. Charlie Pitts is dead, as the voice-over tells us, and Northfield was 'the boys' last ride'. Cole has been shot eleven more times – 'that made twenty-six times in all', yet we watch him painfully drag himself to his feet to the admiring encouragement of the onlookers. 'Ain't that a wonderment!' are his last words. Pinkerton bows his head at the train window; he has arrived too late to dispatch Cole as a common criminal, just in time to see his apotheosis into myth.

The voice-over commentary winds up the story. While Jesse dies in 1882, Cole, after twenty-five years in Stillwater Penitentiary lives on up to 1916: 'He saw a whole new era come into being, but at Northfield his outlaw days had ended.' While the film's relationship to earlier versions of the story is primarily subversive and satirical, it avoids the crude overemphasis of other assaults on the genre, such as *Blazing Saddles* (1974) three years later, and Duvall's drab portrayal of Jesse is as close to the recoverable 'truth' as Tyrone Power's sanitised alternative. Yet Cliff Robertson, co-producer of the movie, makes sure that Cole Younger emerges as the hero of the picture; while so many films of the period were casting a jaundiced eye on the frontier spirit or showing their protagonists locked in the past, he comes up with a surprisingly optimistic and affirmative sense of the future, and the 'wonderments' to come.

The Long Riders

Behind the titles they ride towards us, until the camera picks them up from another angle, the long lens sending them into the distance by the reddish-brown light of the low sun. In contrast to the opening 'disposses-sion' sequence of King's film, or its montage parody in Kaufman's, Hill's heroes are just riding, the shots held together by Ry Cooder's obtrusive guitar and squeezebox soundtrack which largely governs the tone and atmosphere of what follows. 'Missouri – after the civil war ...'. A single laconic title leads abruptly to gunfire and wheeling horses in the street outside a bank. Inside there is silence as the cashier scoops up banknotes. James Keach's Jesse stands centre-frame, a frail, intense figure as stone-faced as Buster Keaton, backed up by his real-life brother Stacy as Frank James. They mount up and wheel away from us round the corner of a building, with again the lens bending the perspective. Further evidence of the self-consciousness of the film's surface comes with the wipe that introduces the next sequence, and one of the sudden changes of pace and mood. Family is a significant theme in the picture, and the casting of four sets of real-life brothers as the James, Youngers, Millers and Fords, if more than a gimmick, might be expected to pay off in some indefinable way. In fact little fraternal warmth comes across; one is more struck by the distance between the characters, as when Jesse and Frank are seen out on the water in a small boat bound for Zee's and attention for his injury, or when Ed, abandoned by the others, is left alone on the shore.

Reviewing *The Long Riders*, Richard Coombs writes of 'camera place-ment which confuses spatial and emotional relationships' (*Monthly Film Bulletin*, September 1980: 178), but this seems deliberate policy on Walter Hill's part. Domestic ties are allowed little of the absolute moral force we encountered in *Jesse James*, where the Major tells Zee that only she can save her husband. In a later sequence, hand in hand, Jesse and Zee (Savannah Smith) are almost lost in the vastness of the countryside which fills the frame. Hill's main addition to the familar story is the introduction of Belle Starr (Pamela Reed) as Cole's lover, self-confidently unashamed of her profession. She may be a whore but, as she says, she 'ain't a cheap one'. Even so, she is not invited to Jesse's wedding, where Bob and Charlie Ford (Nicholas and Christopher Guest) seek admission to the gang, to be rebuffed by the hardened professionals.

We fade to five riders approaching a train and, as in King's film, they bring it to a halt after running along the carriage roofs. Bob Younger's words to the engine driver are an exact quote from the earlier picture: 'I ain't aiming to do nothing. I'm doing it'. Inside Frank calms the passengers with similar politeness: 'Don't worry, ladies and gentlemen. Just taking a permanent loan from the Rock Island payroll'. Indeed, the whole of the sequence recapitulates King's version, as we see posters for a $5,000 reward go up and Pinkerton's men head for the James farm. They are led by Rixley (James Whitmore Jr), a city man like Barshee, but a more serious figure. Two more Pinkertons encounter Jim Younger (Keith Carradine) and his cousin John, and in the ensuing gun battle John is killed, leaving Jim to explain to his family the death of their eighteen-year-old son. The incident, with its forest setting, is reminiscent of the gang's encounter with the widow's landlord in *The Great Northfield Minnesota Raid* and there is the same slow motion camera work as the Pinkertons' man cartwheels from his horse. Although Jim finishes him off as he lies on the ground, it is not presented as the cold-blooded murder of Kaufman's film, but justifiable reprisal. Later, where King's Jesse fulfilled the conventions in 'making them pay', allowing Barshee to draw first, here the gang dispatch the two unarmed Pinkertons' men with a massive display of firepower. The concerted blast lifts them off their feet and backwards in slow motion through a shop window, in an elaborate montage of alternating shots of killers and victims.

It is sometimes suggested that the relative decline in popularity of the western during the 1960s and 1970s was partly due to the fact that it could not match the horror film or science fiction in the level of violence the teenage audience had come to expect. However, in the raid on the barn where the gang take refuge, as Pinkerton's men blast the building full of holes while pigs squeal and die in the mud with whipped pans and subjective shots conveying the panic and confusion, little is left to the imagination.

Hill's film violates fewer of the known facts than the other two examined here, and even the relationship between Cole Younger (David Carradine) and Belle Star has some historical basis. The contrast she offers to the more straightforwardly domestic roles of most of the genre's womenfolk perhaps chimes with the post-feminist present. When her half-Indian husband, Sam Starr, intervenes, and the two men fight over her with Bowie knives, Cole wonders 'What are we fighting for?' 'Nothing both of you ain't already had,' she quips. The scene fades on her pensive, perhaps embittered face. When the gang meet up again for the attempt on the bank at Northfield they are, as in Kaufman's film, entertained by prostitutes, while Jesse waits outside with 'better things to think of'. We cut to the train steaming through the night, with Jim singing while Bob (Robert Carradine) plays a Jew's harp, Frank reading the newspaper and Jesse what looks like a Bible. We see them next mounted in their long grey dusters, riding into Northfield, until Clell Miller cuts through the growing friction: 'Come on, let's take the damned bank'. The camera picks out individual gang members, holding them motionless while the life of the town streams past. There is no calliope but, perhaps in homage to Kaufman's film, a traction engine comes tooting through the frame. Inside the safe is found to be time-locked, and panic and shooting break out.

Bunker, the Elisha Cook character, as in *The Great Northfield Minnesota Raid*, is shot in the back and falls through the glass door into the street.

The raid is a more elaborate sequence than in either of the other films, the colours subdued to browns and violet-greys, the soundtrack mainly composed of gunfire and galloping hooves subjected to weird distortions. In the street the special effects work hard to show us that bullets remove large chunks of body tissue. There is a good deal of Peckinpah-style slow motion, with a man falling from a roof in a montage of a dozen shots before he hits the ground. While Bob tumbles in an ecstasy of pain, firing blindly, the survivors put their horses at a shop window. In slow motion we see the glass shatter, the effect oddly beautiful with repeated low-angle shots of horse and rider sailing over a wall, before returning to the street where Cole picks up his badly wounded brother. Cooder's music gradually feeds into the non-diegetic background noise as we rejoin the gang, riding through a wood, then the sequence finally winds down as the camera scans the tree tops in a subjective shot which takes us to the badly hurt men beneath. Only Jesse is unscathed, and he proposes that Frank and he make their escape, leaving the others to receive medical attention from the pursuing posse. Soon they are lost among the trees, while Bob cries with pain and Clell breathes his last, cursing the 'Goddamned squareheads'. 'Where the hell's Missouri?' wonders Cole, as the bottleneck blues guitar takes us back to Jesse and Frank gloomily approaching the riverside. Jesse is planning a new gang, 'better than ever ... all we gotta do is get home.' 'We never should have left,' Frank answers.

Later, at the prison hospital the sociological and the mythical mingle as the Youngers look back: 'You could say we was drove to it ... if it weren't for the war, we might have been something else.' 'Eleven bullets, must be some kind of record,' the doctor tells Cole. 'Oh hell, we played a rough game. We lost,' is all he says when asked to incriminate the James brothers. But we cut to another location where Rixley is making a deal with the Fords; still boasting they inscribe themselves in a heroic tradition of Missouri heroes: 'James, Younger, Clanton, Earp – now Bob and Charlie Ford.' For $15,000 they will do the job.

Jesse's death asssembles the familiar ingredients. At his home the family are dining, severe and restrained, with Bob and Charlie their guests. When they bring up the subject of another raid, Jesse cuts them short: 'You don't talk business at the table'. When Zee and Beth go out, not 'real fond of the company', he follows them, bending over his son's highchair to say goodnight. Suddenly his eyes alter focus. 'It's crooked,' he says, stepping past them to the picture on the wall: 'I really like this old sampler. Ma gave this to me on our wedding day.' Confident now, the Fords draw their guns. 'I shot Jesse James,' says Bob, writing himself into American history as he pulls the trigger. Behind the final credits we hear the familiar 'Ballad of Jesse James', to pipe and drum accompaniment, before the fiddles join in: 'But history does record, that Bob and Charlie Ford, have laid Jesse James in his grave'.

Hill's film certainly gives us more of the historical record than the others, although there are deliberate inaccuracies, but the emphasis is on style. For John Pym, what unifies the film is 'its tonal shading: its existential sense of characters still managing to function in a limbo of doomed, conscienceless "normality", in the only way they understand' (*Sight and Sound*, Autumn 1980: 267). No doubt this is what Hill is aiming for, and the visual surface engages our attention even while we miss the inventiveness and comedy of Kaufman's version. There, when Remington pronounces, 'They're doomed, doomed' we laugh at his rhetoric; here the gang seem to believe it themselves, the Keaches never cracking their faces as with stoical resignation they succumb to the inevitable. Little remains of the 'deadblameddest buckaroo' commemorated by the Major at the close of the 1939 *Jesse James*.

Hill's film did poorly at the box office, perhaps because of its generally subdued character and the lugubrious presence of James Keach, but more probably because the genre had reached another of its periodic crises. 1980 was the year of its most spectacular commercial failure, Michael Cimino's *Heaven's Gate* , which threatened the survival of the studio itself. We must return to the 1960s, when the way ahead seemed clearer, and large-scale, wide-screen projects like *How the West Was Won* (1962) could guarantee a handsome return for MGM.

4   NEW DIRECTIONS

The commercial success of *How the West Was Won* (1962) helped disguise the fact that there was a marked downturn in the production of westerns at the beginning of the decade, yet Michael Coyne felt justified in claiming that 'qualitatively, 1962 was the genre's most remarkable year' (1998: 106). As several of the leading players entered their sixties, a fashion for reactivating ageing gunfighters who find themselves in a changing world links David Miller's *Lonely Are the Brave*, Ford's *The Man Who Shot Liberty Valance* and Peckinpah's *Ride the High Country*; each released in 1962. A story about 'salvation and loneliness', Peckinpah's film centres on the relationship between former comrades who find themselves on opposite sides of the moral divide. The film foreshadowed the director's subsequent development although for the two stars, Randolph Scott and Joel McCrea, it marked the end of the line. Edward Gallifent discusses other examples of the phenomenon and a sense of loss or contraction within the West itself, 'a natural world that is strangely diminished and unable to sustain itself', in his essay 'Not with a Bang' (Cameron & Pye 1996: 254).

This deglamourised vision is evident in other mid-1960s features, like Tom Gries' *Will Penny* (1967) and even Ford's last western, *Cheyenne Autumn*, handsomely pictorial but lacking energy and with James Stewart contributing a cynically comic Wyatt Earp. The comedy is still broader if mixed with pathos in Elliot Silverstein's *Cat Ballou* (1965), although the out and out parody of Mel Brooks' *Blazing Saddles* was some years away.

Looking back from the vantage point of 1973 Jack Nachbar finds the tradi-tional western formula 'scattered', the tensions and contradictions in Amer-ican society fragmenting the genre: 'heroes are no longer necessarily heroic, the civilised is no longer civilised' (Nachbar 1974: 102).

If the western appeared to be heading in several directions at once, the one that caught the public's attention had its origins in Italy. Sergio Leone did not invent the spaghetti western; indeed, when *A Fistful of Dollars* was completed in 1964 there were difficulties with distribution because the craze which had produced 25 westerns in quick succession was assumed to be past its peak. *Fistful*'s return on its $200,000 investment made it the most successful Italian film to date, and its release in America two years later showed that although initially dismissed as formula entertainment for a more cynical and sophisticated age, as the Italian economic miracle was seen not to be so miraculous after all, the formula had a truly international appeal. Although Leone was a student of the genre and professed admirer of John Ford, as Christopher Frayling (1981) demonstrates in his invaluable study, the Italian western drew on different traditions, and the immediate inspiration for *Fistful* was Kurosawa's *Yojimbo* (1961). Another Kurosawa film, *The Seven Samurai* (1954), had already been remade by John Sturges as *The Magnificent Seven* (1960), but for Leone style took precedence over plot, and Will Wright's attempts to fit the second part of the trilogy, *The Good, the Bad and the Ugly* (1966), partially financed by United Artists and earning enough to qualify for his sample, to the functions of the 'profes-sional plot', are unpersuasive.

At a time when the American western was offering a kind of realism, for example in recognising that it was actually hard to hit anything at a distance with a Colt 45, the Man with No Name announces his arrival by dispatching four opponents in a single burst of fire, while in Tonino Valerii's *My Name is Nobody* (1973), the Terence Hill character indulges in a routine of glass-throwing, fast-drawing and face-slapping only made possible by repeatedly speeding up and re-running the film. The cartoon-like quality of much of the violence, the exhilarating effect of Ennio Morricone's music and the ironic humour might remind us that the same audiences were watching the James Bond films, with Clint Eastwood and Sean Connery competing, as it were, with laconic one-liners and contrasting exhibitions of cool.

For his fourth western, *Once Upon a Time in the West* (1968), an Italian-American co-production, Leone took his cameras to Monument Valley, while Eastwood returned to the States to star in a series of films by Don Siegel before starting to direct his own westerns with *High Plains Drifter* (1972). In a useful appendix on 'The impact of the Spaghettis on the American Western', Frayling takes Peckinpah as the most obvious example, though his characteristic concerns were already established by *Major Dundee* (1964), before he had seen Leone's trilogy. By 1969 however, both he and the American public had absorbed the new influences.

The Wild Bunch

'Without you, I would never have thought of making the films I have made …' (Frayling 1981: 280). If Leone is reporting Peckinpah's acknowledgement accurately this might seem as clear a case of indebtedness as we could wish for, yet Paul Seydor, in the most extensive treatment of Peckinpah's westerns, finds it unnecessary to mention the Italians at all. More significant might be the background in television westerns as scriptwriter and assistant, going back to 1950s favourites like *Gunsmoke* and *The Westerner*. For Will Wright, *The Wild Bunch* is another example of the 'professional plot' (1975: 98), taking its place in the context of a number of 1960s films charting the changeover from a market to a managed economy, seen in the replacement of the classical opposition between the individual and society, where the hero intervenes to protect the community, with the depiction of an elite largely indifferent to the surrounding society. *Rio Bravo* is his first example, but others include Richard Brooks' *The Professionals* (1966), *True Grit* (1969), and *Butch Cassidy and the Sundance Kid*. Certainly the Bunch's appearance behind the credits, riding into Starbuck in their army uniforms to snare drum accompaniment, suggests professionalism, although the military precision with which Pike Bishop (William Holden) has planned the raid on the railway depot soon breaks down in confusion.

In any case it has already been overlaid with more melancholy strains in Jerry Fielding's score and enclosed within the symbolic image of the scorpions tormented by ants. 'If they move, kill 'em,' Pike's first words as they embark on the robbery, discourage sympathetic identification, as does the almost pathological behaviour of Crazy Lee (Bo Hopkins), although when it becomes clear that they are themselves victims of an ambush we want them to escape. The degenerate appearance of the bounty hunters lining the roof sways us further in the same direction. Harrigan, the railroad official who has hired them, is in a tradition of villainous commercial interests going back to the Jesse James story, and his claim to 'represent the law' satisfies us no more than the outraged citizens whose town has been used for a battlefield. In contrast Deke Thornton (Robert Ryan), Pike's former comrade, released from prison on condition that he helps track him down, is allowed the moral high ground. He remains a kind of honorary member of the Bunch in exile throughout, united with them by a common professionalism and respect.

Eluding their pursuers, Pike and his men cross the border to become involved in the Mexican civil war, agreeing to steal a trainload of armaments for General Mapache (Emilio Fernandez) when Angel (Jaime Sanchez), one of their number, kills his own fiancée after finding her in the General's arms. Not all the stolen rifles are handed over; the idealistic Angel begs one case for his revolutionary friends, storing up trouble for the future. In view of the failure of the attempt at Starbuck, the success of the raid on the train – where for once everything goes according to plan, the stolen rifles safely handed over to Mapache's men for the agreed $10,000 – assumes particular importance. It is underlined by the contrast with the incompetence of the pursuing army and the rabble of bounty hunters which is all Deke Thornton has to work with. For Will Wright (1975: 177), drawing on social theorists such as John Kenneth Galbraith and Jürgen Habermas, their professionalism is an aspect of the 'technostructure' which governs contemporary economic relations, with consequential changes in the structure of the myths which carry the new ideology. To this extent the Wild Bunch are in tune with the spirit of the age. Yet it is easier to see them looking back to the way things used to be, before technological

FIGURE 5 *The Wild Bunch*

development – the year is 1913 and the Mexican general has a motor car – and the accompanying social order made their outmoded individualism ever more anachronistic.

Wright sees the professional plot as more concerned with relationships between the heroes than the plot-driven development of the traditional narrative and if, as Jim Kitses claims, the Bunch have 'no honour, only a way of life that is shared' (1969: 165), the way of life does generate a kind of value system, although initially it is subjected to irony. Some of the famous lines taken out of context can be made to represent a mindless machismo, but the surrounding texture usually qualifies them. Even the Gorches (Warren Oates and Ben Johnson) come to admire Angel's courage: he had 'guts', he 'played his string out to the end' in refusing to admit to Mapache's men that he took the rifles with the connivance of the Bunch, while Pike's austere code, which he clings to even when it works against them, is set against the situational ethics of Dutch (Ernest Borgnine), for Peckinpah 'the moral conscience of the group' (Seydor 1980: 85).

Although the Mexican setting might suggest another point of comparison with the Italian westerns, Peckinpah's long-time personal enthusiasm for the country is well attested. While the Gorches see it as no different from Texas, the flowing waters of the Rio Grande and shady trees on the opposite side tell another story. When they reach Agua Verde, Angel's village, music and song salve their wildness, with the Gorches deferring to the womenfolk and Dutch and even Old Man Sykes joining the dance. A patriarchal village elder explains: 'We all dream of being a child again. Even the worst of us – perhaps the worst most of all.' Of course it is an impossible dream, and the protracted scene in which the Bunch ride out next day to the strains of 'Adelita', hands raised in salute, gives the farewell a ritualistic quality. In any case – for Mexico too, as the white bearded elder acknowledges – 'these are the years of sadness'. Our first shot of the village reveals a starving dog and ruined buildings, and if we see only women, children, and old men it is because the Federales have raided it, with Angel's father one of their victims.

A single shot, of a woman breastfeeding her baby with a bandolier slung across her chest, reinforces the point that the feminine offers no simple refuge from masculine compulsions. It takes us to Agua Verde, the heart of Mapache territory where the Federales strut about, presided over by their drunken, be-medalled general, for Terence Butler (1979) a figure of patri- archal oppression. Yet as usual Peckinpah, even while he employs stock types as the general's entourage (the shy Zamora, the comical Herrera, the stiffly militaristic Germans) complicates the simpler oppositions: in effect there are many Mexicos. The political struggle between Villa's revolution- aries and the corrupt Federales is another aspect of the country and in the person of Angel becomes part of the dynamics of the Bunch. However, the Villistas remain silent, shadowy figures, the film not presuming to compre- hend their impersonal concerns within the 'simple story about bad men in changing times'. Although Deke and Sykes (Edmond O'Brien) will ride with them, it is for the excitement and comradeship which they can still only find outside the law.

If the spaghettii westerns seem preoccupied with style, Peckinpah communicates his vision through texture, the overloaded image created in Lucien Ballard's richly expressive camerawork challenging and disturbing the viewer. Paul Seydor's chapter on *The Wild Bunch* notices how the telephoto lens has the effect of compressing the depth of field, bringing us close up against events, while the habitual use of zoom and reverse zoom prevents us from adopting a comfortably detached perspective on the story as it unfolds (Seydor 1980: 115). Peckinpah's most readily identifiable trademark, the intercutting between slow motion and normal time, again has the effect of exposing us to more information than we could absorb through conventional editing while retaining the immediacy of actual events.

The use of flashbacks is governed by similar considerations, filling us in on necessary plot information but also illustrating the psychological processes of the characters. They can also be used to make connections between them, as in the recall of Deke's capture as a result of Pike's carelessness, when the editing suggests that this is a joint memory for the two men, each recollecting it from a different location and with different emotions. Indeed, the way in which the past is always there, inescapably present, is part of the oppressive feeling of the film, only occasionally relieved by laughter or physical action. Even the music adds to this effect, quite without the exhilaration of the Morricone scores, only in the Mexican village breaking free into an expansive melody. 'Shall we gather at the river' is hard and astringent in this version, and elsewhere the muted brass, spare orchestral texture, and insistent drums create tension and unease or suddenly fall silent. For the interior of the railroad office an amplified heartbeat takes over, as though we were trapped inside a Poe short story. The structure reinforces this impression, since after the escape from Starbuck the Bunch are on the run. Although the posse never catches up with them, ruling out the expected confrontation, their persistence still works to reduce Pike's options.

Although the professional plot is characterised by multiple heroes where in Wright's phrase 'their shared shared status and skill become the basis for mutual respect and affection' (1975: 86) there is never any doubt that Pike is the leader. His leg wound is clearly significant and even symbolic. He received it in the excised scene with Aurora, the one woman who has been significant for him, from her vengeful husband who then killed her, and it recalls the moment in *Major Dundee* when the Major, off-duty for once, bathes in the life-giving waters with Teresa, only to take an Indian arrow in the thigh. Women seem to expose men at their most vulnerable, and sexual encounters are often succeeded by self-disgust. One hesitates to write this off as simple misogyny; the flaws are part of the hero's own make-up.

In Terence Butler's Freudian study, Peckinpah's world is haunted by a nightmare figure of the father, crippling the hero's emotional development from the start (see Butler 1979: 29). The violent outburst becomes a frustrated gesture against the forces of repression, finding relief at last in the assault on Mapache and his men. For Butler of course, repressed homosexuality underlies the all-male group. Pike's passivity before Deke on the two occasions – at the bank and the bridge – when zooms show the two men aware of each other, with Deke's gun trained on his quarry, he sees as 'an unconscious yearning for Thornton's bullets to penetrate his body' (1979: 55). Our attention perhaps goes rather to Deke's inability to pull the trigger, prompted by an easily understandable reluctance to kill a friend. He never wavers in his admiration for Pike and seems not to blame him for his capture. Which does not mean that Pike is not at least half in love with easeful death; Deke is a part of his own past which he is running away from. Certainly Holden is good at conveying Pike's doubt and self-division and an authority which doesn't depend on moral rectitude. By this stage in the film his catalogue of failures is already long; with Deke's capture, Aurora's death, and the failure of the raid on Starbuck. The decision to let Angel take the rifles, thus breaking the agreement with Mapache, proves to be another, and his inability to protect his man from the Mexican general's revenge becomes the most public challenge to the code he had adumbrated earlier.

When *The Wild Bunch* was released the question of violence was the one that most exercised the critics. Its indiscriminate and unpredictable nature, escaping the confines of instrumentality which presume to order it, are emphasised as the bounty hunters' fire brings down soldiers and citizens. It never becomes the turkey shoot which acts as the climax of *Rio Bravo*. The slow motion inserts of bodies falling through the air have a balletic grace, but in aestheticising the violence they do not anaesthetise us to its impact. Although the blood bags burst, the rapidity of the cutting gives us no chance to linger, and we never have the extended sequences of systematically inflicted brutality to which Eastwood is subjected in the *Dollars* trilogy (1964–68). The kinetic energy of the violent scenes is what strikes us, and if feeling is momentarily divorced from sensation, the total effect, as Seydor explains (1980: 116), depends on our being simultaneously involved and detached.

In the light of later screen violence, like that in *Reservoir Dogs* (1992), it is hard to convict Peckinpah of excess. The gap between art and life remains, and only an inappropriate literal-mindedness could confuse the implied viewer's willing suspension of horror with the 'real' viewer's moral approval. As Pike and the Bunch select their targets in the pause after Angel dies, we accept that the violence is directed at figures of authority, even our traditional enemies, the Germans on Mapache's staff, and in what follows they seem as much victims as the soldiers and villagers who die in the hail of bullets. But they have exercised a choice.

Whether or not Pike believes his own arguments when he proposes the return to Agua Verde as a safe haven from the pursuing posse, it is difficult to believe they will escape a second time. The sound of the fiesta as they ride in functions as an ironic reprise of the music and song at Angel's village; this time he is the prime attraction, his body still towed behind the red car. However hopeless the situation, some response is called for. As Pike had argued earlier: 'When you side with a man you stay with him, and if you don't, you're like some animal; you're finished – we're finished – all of us.'

'Let's go,' the words with which he breaks the silence, get the expected answer: 'Why not?' The walk to the square after we see them collecting their weapons reintroduces the snare drum rhythm of the opening credits as the work comes full circle. This is not the sterilised, stylised confrontation of the Leone westerns; the scene is filled with people who will soon be implicated in the result of their decision. The farewell song from Angel's village joins the drum on the soundtrack, less harmoniously than before, more bitter than sweet. The drums reach a crescendo then cut out suddenly as they come face to face with Mapache (as usual the initial shot is followed by a zoom bringing us closer): 'What d'you want?' 'We want Angel.' For a moment it seems he might agree, as their battered companion is pulled to his feet. But in a final brutal joke, Mapache cuts his throat. The second before he does so they realise his intention and we cut to Dutch's horrified reaction before Pike shoots him dead.

The ensuing pause as the Mexicans back away, half-raising their hands, might conceivably have been translated into escape, but we are not to be denied our violent catharsis. The pause, apparently not in the original screenplay, introduces the element of choice which gives their deaths significance. Once the high command are out of the way, the battle resolves itself into a struggle for possession of the machine gun. Earlier we have seen the Bunch present it to Mapache, and his attempts to use it without the tripod send his own followers tumbling for cover. A symbol of power, blatantly phallic in character, its rhythm dominates the montage of the next few minutes. Even Deke Thornton, watching the scene through his binoculars, is allowed a kind of vicarious participation. Something might be made of the fact that only Dutch is denied a chance to wield the awesome weapon. Even in what is essentially men's business, the women are every-where, silently reproachful or caught up as shields, and finally it is a woman who shoots Pike in the back. 'Bitch!' he gasps, killing her in retaliation, but we need not see this as the ultimate betrayal or even evidence of the direc-tor's misogyny, any more than we should deduce a dislike of children from the fact that a boy scarcely able to hold his rifle inflicts another wound. However affirmatively we see Pike's final moments – and for Butler 'the flood-gates of love open up in his personality' (1979: 60) – he is a carrier of death, and the forces of life must drive him out.

We elide to the aftermath of the struggle, with Fielding's music at its most potent and elegiac. 'The strange thing is,' Peckinpah said, 'that you feel a great sense of loss when these killers reach the end of the line' (cited in Seydor 1980: 107). A pan shows us vultures waiting along the rooftops as the posse picks its way through the dust to its prey. Deke finds Pike, still clutching the grip of the machine gun, its barrel angled upwards, and in a spaghetti-sized close-up takes the gun from his holster; a senti-mental keepsake or evidence of his own 're-phallicising' as a result of Pike's heroism? The others ride out, the bodies of the dead slung over their saddles, but gunfire in the distance tells us they have not got far, and this is confirmed when Old Man Sykes arrives with the Indians and the patriarch from Angel's village. Although these are the forces of the revolution they coincide with the flow of women, children, and wounded out of Agua Verde; dispossessed refugees. If the Bunch have struck a blow for freedom they have also inflicted wanton destruction on the Mexicans. We are not permitted a simply positive political vision, although we see the machine gun commandeered by the Villistas. Sykes' invitation to Deke to join them is deliberately low-key: 'Me and the boys here, we've got some work to do. Do you want to come along? It ain't like it used to be, but it will do.' As Sykes and Deke are united in laughter, lap dissolves take us to the laughter of the Bunch in the aftermath of Starbuck and then to the sequence of their leaving Angel's village, with the song 'Adelita' once more, this time warm and with plaintive harmonies restored. They have become figures of myth, comrades who gave their lives to defend a friend and won the battle against overwhelming odds. The camera pulls back as a freeze-frame gives us our final view of the shadowy figures moving easily under the shade trees, the gore and pain purged away, the stuff of legend and romance: the Wild Bunch.

Although the film was eventually successful, both critically and commercially, Peckinpah was to continue to have difficulties with his projects, and the two westerns still to come, *The Ballad of Cable Hogue* (1969) and *Pat Garrett and Billy the Kid* (1973) – if highly personal – are less convincing than *The Wild Bunch*. For many critics it remains peculiarly 'emblematic of modern America' (Coyne 1997: 161) and of a decade when assassinations at home and massacres abroad soured the dream. Vietnam, as refracted through Ralph Nelson's *Soldier Blue* (1970), even invaded one of the oldest components of the myth, the dispossessed Native Americans, and it is to them that we turn next.

5   THE INDIANS

Although the Native Americans have appeared in westerns from the beginning, since history is usually written by the victors it has most often been as the villains duly defeated in the last reel. Yet whether we take the simple collocation of cowboys and Indians or the more sophisticated binary opposition between civilisation and the wilderness, their role is central to the genre. The stereotypes and the dramatic possibilities they provide date back at least to James Fenimore Cooper, writing at a time when their history was still in the making, their eventual defeat and the white man's guilt over how it came about still in the future. Cooper was already troubled by what he saw, in some ways more so than Michael Mann in the latest remake of *The Last of the Mohicans,* which dispenses with Cora's racially mixed parentage and promotes Natty to conventional romantic hero. Incidentally, in giving him an adoptive Indian father and brother it brings him closer to the situation in *Little Big Man* (1970), although he draws from the two cultures an assurance, a firm sense of identity, which Jack Crabb never really achieves.

There were 'good' Indians in earlier Hollywood films, and sometimes Native American actors were cast to play them, although often – like Hollywood negroes – they were condemned to present a caricature of themselves, with the leading roles reserved for whites. Even *Broken Arrow* (1950), the film in which Delmer Daves is usually considered to have initiated a new respect for the Indian side of the story, has Jeff Chandler as Cochise and Debra Paget as his daughter, paying for her marriage to James Stewart with death. As Ralph and Natasha Friar observe in their readable and compendious account of Hollywood's treatment of the Indian, 'audiences were grabbed by their throats and large liberal doses of a new patent medicine were rammed down their gullets' (Friar & Friar 1972: 202). In *Broken Lance* (1954) Sol Siegel has Katy Jurado as the Indian princess, nobly trying to mitigate Spencer Tracey's aggression but tactfully fading into the natural background as their son and his white bride begin a new life. Robert Wagner, as the son, is not the treacherous half-breed of countless western stories, and in *The Searchers* the Cherokee blood in Martin Pawley's veins seems to inoculate him against the racist prejudices of his 'Uncle' Ethan. That film is an interesting amalgam of old and new attitudes to the Indian, with Ethan's antagonist, the cruel but charismatic Scar, played by Henry Brandon, and Martin's Comanche 'wife' Look, by a Mexican, although the traditional image of the Indian maiden is still provided by Natalie Wood, admittedly a white girl captured by Scar's tribe. In *She Wore a Yellow Ribbon* Ford had already paired John Wayne in friendship with the imposing Chief Big Tree and foregone the usual slaughter of the Indians, content to defuse the situation by running off their ponies. His final western, *Cheyenne Autumn*, if far from his best, at least attempts a sympathetic portrait of the dispossessed Indians' long march, based on Mari Sandoz's historical novel of the same name, although again the stars were white.

If the soldiers who accompany the Cheyenne out of Oklahoma are less admirable than those of Ford's earlier cavalry trilogy, they are not the sadistic killers of Ralph Nelson's *Soldier Blue* (1970) a few years later, by which time the demythologising process is well under way. Other films of the period, like Polonsky's *Tell Them Willie Boy is Here* (1969) and Silverstein's *A Man Called Horse* (1970) are potentially more exacting treatments of the clash of cultures, although again the leading roles did not go to the Indians, who according to the Friars still saw themselves travestied, however well-intentioned the film-makers.

Arthur Penn's first film had been a western, *The Left-Handed Gun*, a version of the Billy the Kid story with Paul Newman and lots of Freudian darkness, and more recently *The Missouri Breaks*, with Marlon Brando and Jack Nicholson, confirmed his feeling for the genre. His adaptation of Thomas Berger's award-winning 1964 novel 'Little Big Man' provided a substantial role for Chief Dan George, and although never intended as a documentary, accurately reflects 1960s liberal attitudes to the events of the 1860s and 1870s. 'I was interested in the picture,' claimed Dustin Hoffman, 'because it presents the Indian in a different light.'

Little Big Man

This new attitude is established in the framing device, carried over from the novel's 'Foreword by a Man of Letters', where what follows is introduced as the tape-recorded recollections of the sole survivor of the Battle of Little Big Horn, Jack Crabb, now 121-years-old. Hoffman's elaborately antiquated make-up and quavering voice lay bare the device as thoroughly as the scarlet letter Hawthorne claimed to have discovered in the custom house, and we settle back, not for the unvarnished truth but a fictional recreation of some of the known facts. The blurb of the novel offers 'as authentic an account of the redman's way of life as any paleface will ever write' and one assumes that Berger has done his research on Cheyenne customs. Yet the satirical mode is excused literal realism, and the death of Wild Bill Hickok, Custer's raid on Cheyenne encampments by the Wichita River in 1868, and his defeat at the Little Big Horn eight years later are the only 'historical' events we witness.

As useful for Penn's purposes are the hundreds of westerns we have seen, so that although one can, as does Leo Braudy, describe Crabb in the course of his long life as 'acting out all the possiblities for a man in the Old West' (1971: 32), many of the possibilities take the form of scenes from the movies. When Crabb takes Custer's advice to go west, the Indian attack on the coach which follows with comic immediacy on the General's 'personal guarantee' of safety recapitulates Ford's *Stagecoach*, with Jack doing the John Wayne stunt along the backs of the galloping horses, and the Donald Meek-lookalike minister taking an arrow in the chest.

The lack of a more structured plot is one reason why Wright (1975) finds the film embarrassing to his categories. Another is the absence of a conventional hero, since throughout Jack is more acted upon than acting, although this is true of Berger's novel, where he wanders back and forth between the Cheyenne and the whites as chance dictates. In a thoughtful analysis of the differences between book and film reprinted in *Western Movies* (Pilkington & Graham 1979), John W. Turner sees the savagery/civilisation opposition structuring both, but in the film the contrast is insufficiently sustained because the inherent naturalism of the medium privileges the sceptical, empirical values of the civilised world over the magical, intuitive world of the Indian. Certainly the film has fewer defences against a tendency to sentimentalise the Cheyenne, and the Jack of Berger's novel who can say, 'Indians sure made me sick. I could hardly breathe for the smell inside my own house, where them sloppy women I supported stirred up the muck we was going to eat for supper' never makes an appearance on the screen.

The opening massacre, where we pan to the burning wagons on the empty plain, picked out with the sharp clarity of a Remington painting, complemented by the wry, self-aware guitar and harmonica on the soundtrack before the titles, introduces this tendency at the outset. Jack's childhood with the tribe is unequivocally paradisial: 'I wasn't just playing Indians, I was living Indians'.

In spite of the voice-over recall that introduces it, Jack's first period with the Cheyenne involves quite conventional Indian material. Yet already Penn is preparing the ground for its later development as an attractive counterculture – the bluesy, Sonny Terry-Brownie McGee-type soundtrack helps too – with the Cheyenne tolerant and non-violent to a degree, while the name the tribe give themselves, 'The Human Beings', informs us from the start where true humanity is to be found. Only when the hunting party returns to find their camp burnt out and the women and children killed by the army does Lodge Skins retaliate, and then his method of warfare is 'kinda pitiful', with coup-sticks against the cavalry's carbines. Penn does not choose to tell us, as Berger does, of these same women and children mutilating the enemy dead.

FIGURE 6 *Little Big Man*

When the sequence ends, with Jack revealing that he is white as one of the troopers is about to kill him ('God bless George Washington,' the words pop out), it is as if he has been playing Indians after all, his years with the Cheyenne seemingly having had no effect on his command of his original language. So he returns to civilisation, in the form of the Reverend Pendrake and his young wife (Fay Dunaway). Pendrake has a totally bigoted view of the Indian, and wants to beat the devil out of him, while Mrs Pendrake's concern for his spiritual and physical welfare scarcely conceals her nymphomaniac tendencies. Ford's favourite, 'Shall We Gather at the River', is the hymn she sings while sponging his back, by now the genre's shorthand for dubious revivalist sentiment. Her attempts at biblical instruction ('Jesus was a gentile, like us') are as fanciful as Lodge Skins' legends, although without the moral coherence. Jack's religious enthusiasm, we are told, is genuine, but puberty clearly has a good deal to do with it and his 'religious period' comes to an abrupt end when he catches Mrs Pendrake *in flagrante* with the storekeeper.

We are not asked to accept any of the participants as believable figures, nor are we offered examples elsewhere in the film of religious belief as a legitimate source of values. Lodge Skins' opinion that the white men 'do not know where the centre of the earth is' goes unchallenged, and there is no pretence of serious debate; the comedy is to be sufficient, if not perhaps for repeated viewing.

To extend the critique of white society Penn introduces Alardyce Merriweather, the mountebank patent medicine dealer whose honesty initially at least Jack finds refreshing after Mrs Pendrake's hypocrisy. The whole episode involves only four minutes of screen time and is interrupted by the reappearance of Jack's sister Caroline, now grotesquely masculine in manner although offering him what he has never known, 'a real family life'. Penn underlines the paradox by cutting from her self-definition as 'the bosom of your family' to gunfire as she teaches him to shoot. Violence and sexual disorientation have invaded the most intimate of human relationships.

Under her guidance Jack enters his 'gunfighter period', but with the intervention of another tutelary figure, Wild Bill Hickok, discovers that he has no stomach for blood. More broad comedy details the collapse of his business as storekeeper when his partner defaults, and the loss of his wife Olga, carried off by the Indians. We are ready for the action to switch once more to the Cheyenne, given the alternating structure of the narrative, but first we see General Custer, on horseback with the sun back-lighting his golden hair. In the novel he does not appear until the Washita River masssacre, and in presenting him here, the low-angle camera reproducing Jack's admiring gaze, Penn is perhaps proposing a choice between competing father-figures to clarify the main lines of his theme. From the start, however, we are invited to distance ourselves from Jack's enthusiasm. Played by Richard Mulligan, Custer is handsome enough but his habitual rhetoric, his vanity, and his overweening self-confidence (repeatedly shown to be unjustified) are always in evidence. In contrast, Lodge Skins' quiet eloquence and visionary intuition are vindicated by events. Jack tries to counter his opinion that all white men are 'crazy' by citing Custer as an exception, 'as brave as any human being' but, as the film presents him, he is the craziest of them all.

It is Custer who brings to an end Jack's life with the Cheyenne after he has taken an Indian wife, Sunshine – a true man of the 1960s, he proves more adept at love than war – on the banks of the Washita River, the stretch of land granted the Indians by President and Congress, as idyll gives way to history. Penn's treatment of the massacre is the high point of the film, eerily beautiful as the column of horsemen appear in long shot on the snow-covered plain. As they ride among the tepees and the slaughter begins, the drums and pipes get louder and we see through the haze of the camp-fires the band in the distance, playing throughout. The tune is 'Garry Owen', associated with Custer in Raoul Walsh's *They Died With Their Boots On* (1941). Penn says he did not want the massacre to be too documentary, or too absolutely gory, but inevitably at this date audiences were reminded of news photographs from Vietnam, as we see the Asiatic features of the young girls running from the flames, and the culmination of the scene in the death of Sunshine and her child, repeatedly fired on by a trooper, is gory enough.

It is difficult to disagree with John Turner's argument (see Pilkington & Graham 1979) that if this is the structural fulcrum of the story we expect more of a change in what follows, not least in the character of Jack himself, whereas what we get is really more of the same. With some ingenuity Penn, and his scriptwriter Calder Willingham, develop Jack's attempted revenge on Custer (equally abortive in the novel but soon forgotten) to explain the self-disgust which motivates his subsequent actions, culminating in withdrawal from all society and finally taking him to the verge of suicide. He is only reprieved by the chance arrival of Custer and the Seventh Cavalry in the run-up to the Little Big Horn.

By now Richard Mulligan's Custer is recapitulating the tradition of crazed military men, like Sterling Hayden in *Dr Stangelove* (1963) or Robert Duval in *Apocalypse Now* (1979), after days in the saddle suffering from 'poison from the gonads'. His contrariness causes him to recognise Jack, in spite of his earlier attempt to assassinate him, as a potential 'reverse barometer'. Thus Jack is allowed to play an active part in his downfall, securing his revenge simply by telling the truth, which the General interprets as a double bluff, so leading his men to destruction at the hands of the waiting Indians.

The traditional western hero, whose actions set the world to rights, has no place here, where inexorable historical forces dictate the final outcome. As Lodge Skins recognises, there is 'an endless supply' of white men but only 'a limited number of Human Beings'. For this reason 'it is a good day to die', the phrase he uses throughout. The film reproduces much of his moving valedictory speech, as Jack leads him to the hill-top, but then Penn makes a decision which has troubled the critics. 'He laid down on the damp rocks and died right away,' we read on the last page before the editor's epilogue, but in the film 'the magic doesn't work' and as the rain begins to fall he wakes up, in comic disgust to find himself still in the land of the living. This ending, Turner maintains, 'undermines the dignity of Old Lodge Skins' (Pilkington & Graham 1979: 120) and defuses the tragic logic of the Indians' ultimate defeat. One can only reply that Penn is not aiming at tragedy, whatever the historical circumstances may seem to require, and that Lodge Skins' charm and appetite for life, rather than his noble suffering, are what appeal to us. With his new Snake wife, Doesn't Like Horses, the future is still so interesting that Paradise does not seem completely lost. Only the white man with his straight lines demands the finality of the closed ending; for the Indian, as he tells Jack in the novel, 'there is no permanent winning or losing when things move, as they should, in a circle'.

Penn says that Jack emerges with 'a certain detached view', and it could be that the death of Sunshine is too immediate, as presented in the film, to make that detachment tenable. Berger's novel may be blacker, although there too the blackness is modified by the comic structure. The final shot of the film has Hoffman, head-in-hand in the darkening hospital ward, with more wrinkles than Lodge Skins at his oldest. 'I didn't know,' apologises the editor, as he packs up his tape-recorder. Perhaps we do not know more about the Indians or the real Little Big Horn than we did before. As usual with Penn's films, the focus on violence and its kinetic properties does not imply any deep emotional involvement. We too remain detached, admiring the craftsmanship, but there is no pretence, any more than in *Bonnie and Clyde*, of getting inside the period depicted. The film may be 'beyond any doubt the most advanced document in the process of re-evaluating [the western's] sacred myths, a work of art in the cause of peace and understanding' (Fenin & Everson 1977: 370) but only by substituting still newer myths of its own.

Ulzana's Raid

If Penn's film explicitly redefined the Indians as human beings rather than the faceless savages of colonial history, thus questioning the progressive view of the white advance, other anti-progressive westerns took a different line. In the early 1950s Robert Aldrich's third feature film, *Apache* (1954), had also taken a sympathetic view of the Indian, in the person of the lone Apache, played by Burt Lancaster, on the run from white civilisation but with no real alternative elsewhere. The original script called for his death at the hands of the federal authorities. His courage, as Aldrich explained in interview, was to be measured against the inevitable, but the studio ending, finally acceded to by Lancaster, let him live. Other westerns – *Vera Cruz* (1954) and *Four for Texas* (1963) – followed, but Aldrich returned to the question of the Indians only with *Ulzana's Raid* in 1972. Again Burt Lancaster was involved, this time as McIntosh the white scout, but with the help of an intelligent and literate script from Alan Sharp, Aldrich produced one of his best films and one of the most thoughtful accounts of the clash of cultures.

The title sequence sets up the opposition as we see Ulzana (Joaquin Martinez) breaking out of the San Carlos reservation with nine of his followers, filmed in close-up and semi-darkness among the horses they are stealing. Ethnic music, featuring flutes and percussion, alternates with more abrasive conventional orchestral scoring. The leftward pan along the horses' backs is continued in the next shot, where we approach Fort Lowell accompanied by 'pastoral' strains, although latrines standing out on the plain puncture the mood and jaunty military music takes over. The off-duty soldiers are playing baseball, a purposeless rule-based activity compared with horse-stealing, and the young Lieutenant DeBuin (Bruce Davison) is umpiring, incompetently but imperturbably, a source of friction with the men which will resurface later in the film.

A galloping rider brings news that Ulzana has broken out and the reaction among the commanding officers takes a form familiar from other cavalry pictures, the letter of the regulations set against the common sense need for immediate action. Here the major insists on discovering the exact number of the war party before dispatching troops in pursuit, thus giving Ulzana four hours start as McIntosh points out. On the other hand he is not a martinet figure (like Fonda's Colonel Thursday in *Fort Apache*) but a humane and sympathetic man, out of his depth in the circumstances, unable to understand the Apaches, helplessly holding up the rule book – helplessness in fact seems a principal motif in the film: there are no heroes or villains.

McIntosh's role is familiar enough too, his civilian costume separating him from the military men. 'He's very forthright,' as DeBuin says. 'A wilful and opinionated man,' replies the officer. 'He knows the Apaches which I can freely confess is more than I do.' This covers most of the ingredients, and Lancaster's laconic, understated manner is traditional in the western hero. One can hear John Wayne saying many of the same lines, and indeed one sometimes has. His later comments on the Apaches' ability to get maximum mileage out of their ponies is almost verbatim from *The Searchers*.

In this sequence we are also given enough information about DeBuin to understand how he will function to focus the issues the film goes on to engage. His father, it seems, is a minister who believes that 'a lack of Christian feeling is at the root of our problems with the Indians'. The major's observation that in taking command of the detail to track down Ulzana he will have an opportunity to test some of his father's theories emphasises the highly schematic organisation of what follows.

The first explicit violence in the film comes when Ulzana's party attack the trooper accompanying Mrs Rukeyser, the wife of one of the settlers, and her son back to the fort. His initial impulse seems to be to escape

FIGURE 7 *Ulzana's Raid*

but he turns to answer her cries for help – by shooting her dead and
taking up the boy. When his horse is shot from under him he turns the
gun on himself. The sequence is shocking in its rapidity and in what it
implies about the suffering, the fate-worse-than-death thus avoided. As
the Indians move on to attack Rukeyser's farm the contrast is between
his bravado as he barricades himself in, shouting defiance, and the
impersonal, almost clinical efficiency of Ulzana's plot to lure him out. We
are introduced to the sequence through the 'long glasses', the binoculars
Ulzana uses as he supervises the attack. Throughout, he is usually at a
distance from the action, and here it is the white man's military tactics
that seem 'kinda pitiful' as we see his dog shot full of arrows and the
cabin set on fire, before the bugle call apparently announcing the cavalry
riding to the rescue brings him out into the open. His heartfelt relief
– 'God! God! You take all the praise and all the glory' – is brilliantly
juxtaposed with a shot of a bugle carried by one of the troopers, still some
way from the farm. The notion of Christian providence, which links with
DeBuin's personal quest, is questioned here even more fundamentally.
Both the bugle and the binoculars are part of a complex series of motifs

at the level of plot, articles which the Indians take from the whites, agents of civilisation yet used to subvert it.

When the cavalry eventually reach the scene and camp for the night, the men discuss the significance of what they are involved with around the fire, confirming the pattern of alternating action sequences, expertly shot but without the overt excitement of more conventional chase westerns, and verbal exploration of the issues. DeBuin asks the questions: 'Why are your people like that? Why are they so cruel?' The answers come from Ke-Ni-Tay (Sorge Luke) the Indian scout, who begins to emerge as one of the central characters. In interview Aldrich suggests that he might have appeared still more strongly had commercial considerations not required Lancaster to figure as the star. Ke-Ni-Tay is in fact Ulzana's brother-in-law, and on one level the good Indian to his bad. Even here we can recognise the 'splitting' often seen in the handling of the Indian from Fenimore Cooper onwards. Ke-Ni-Tay's calm, dignified manner, his total competence and trustworthiness, give him some of the qualities of the noble savage, but as he explains to DeBuin, he too could kill and torture as Ulzana does.

The justification depends on the idea of power; the Apaches kill to take strength from their victims, and the more protracted the suffering, the more power is to be obtained: 'Here, in this land, man must have power'. The torture then is not meaningless sadism; as he demonstrates with the analogy of the fire, the longer it lasts the greater benefit they can derive from it. The highly schematic nature of the debate is clear when DeBuin takes up the question with McIntosh. When asked if he hates the Apache, he answers that to do so would be like hating the desert ''cause there ain't no water on it'. Like Ke-Ni-Tay he accepts the situation as he finds it. 'After all, they are men, made in God's image like ourselves,' DeBuin persists when next day Sergeant Burns finds him reading the Bible his father has given him. Yet as Burns suggests, the doctrine of an eye for an eye is 'the only fix you're going to get on the Apache'.

In addition to the fully articulated debate simple juxtaposition without comment is used to enrich the texture, as when Ke-Ni-Tay, filtering the water Ulzana has polluted with the blood of one of the ponies which has gone lame watches DeBuin elaborately cleaning his teeth. One could compare the subtlety of the technique here with the more obvious dissension in a film released the same year with a rather similar theme, Michael Winner's *Chato's Land* (1971). There too we have a range of attitudes in the posse pursuing the half-breed Chato (Charles Bronson), ranging from the restraint of Quine, the sympathetic Confederate captain (Jack Palance) to the rabid racism of his followers. Like Ulzana, Chato remains remote, rarely speaking and when he does, only in Apache. His cruel efficiency raises few moral problems, since he kills only in self-defence, and once the posse have found his hideout and violated his wife, the narrative adopts the pattern of rape and reprisal Winner and Bronson were to repeat in the *Death Wish* films (1974–85) a few years later.

In Aldrich's film, the struggle is more evenly balanced; Ulzana remains a man like us, even while the differences are insisted on. We never get behind his impassive eyes, but the death of his son clearly moves him; we assume it is the reason he makes no attempt to escape when finally cornered. The way the film is assembled underlines the pattern of similarity and difference, the parallel syntax acting to separate events rather than combining them in a coherent narrative. If one remembers *The Naked Spur*, when Ben fires his rifle after killing Jesse we cut away to see Howie and Roy mounting up, then back to Ben and Lena waiting, the conventional method of telling a story in film. Here there is much more frequent intercutting than narrative continuity requires, and instead of a form of accelerated montage as seen so often in the western, building tension as the cavalry ride to the rescue, here it simply emphasises the failure of the two worlds to gel. The detail of the cavalry bugle already mentioned, where the cut does not indicate simultaneity but picks up the troop further forward in time, about to discover Rukeyser's body, is one example. Another comes in the sequence where DeBuin mistakes sun catching the Indian look-out's binoculars for the signal agreed with Ke-Ni-Tay, setting off too soon to join the others and so aborting the planned rescue. It seems impossible to get the timing right.

Under the strain of the situation and denied the confidence of his men, the lieutenant shows signs of mounting hysteria, brought to a head when he catches the troopers mutilating the body of Ulzana's son. 'You don't like to think of white men behaving like Indians, it kind of confuses the issue,' McIntosh spells it out for us. Again he acts as his guide and counsellor, advising him to stop hating and start thinking. Aldrich engineers plenty of obstacles in the way of this process, even exaggerating the crimes of the Apaches rather than falling into line with more liberal contemporary views. 'Apaches usually rape women to death,' McIntosh explains when they find Mrs Riordan reduced to madness by her ordeal, and they have spared her only to present the army with another tactical problem. Ke-Ni-Tay and McIntosh discuss possible lines of action with DeBuin, but the final decision has to be his.

Nachbar draws attention to the parallels between DeBuin and Ke-Ni-Tay, seeing them as sharing similar personal problems. Both are outsiders in the main body of the troop, and suffer from a 'mutually shared neurosis' (Pilkington & Graham 1979: 144). If, however, the Indian is troubled, his impassive features betray no sign of it; certainly we see none of the overtly neurotic behaviour Mann shows us in Howie Kemp's pursuit of Ben. Why exactly Ke-Ni-Tay should take the white man's money to track down his own people is never made clear, nor whether it is a source of puzzlement to himself. Whatever his relationship with Ulzana, Aldrich needs him in the film primarily as spokesman for the Indians' way of thinking, and his final confrontation with the older man seems to exclude us from anything they have between them. Incidentally, in avoiding the fight to the death which the conventions of the genre lead us to expect, it denies us the excitement of a climax and serves to maintain the separation of pursuers and pursued. Only another Apache gets to kill Ulzana; there is no cathartic victory for the white man.

The failure of DeBuin's plan – which leaves half his command wiped out and McIntosh mortally wounded – means there is no real victory at all. He does accede to his request that he be left to die in peace, even if it is 'not Christian', rather than making a futile attempt to get him to a surgeon, and the army forms – 'Mr McIntosh', 'Mr DeBuin' – signal a new respect which extends to Ke-Ni-Tay too. If the social niceties are a refuge from something more bleakly nihilistic, Aldrich does not seem to be offering them ironically, any more than is Ford in John Wayne's defence of Colonel Thursday at the close of *Fort Apache*. In any case, DeBuin is prepared to take the initiative in allowing Ke-Ni-Tay to bury his brother-in-law rather than taking the body back to the fort as army regulations require. He has moved beyond hatred, and although McIntosh's laconic 'Never mind, you'll learn' specifically refers to the rolling of cigarettes, it clearly has a more general application and is a form of commendation, coming from the older and wiser man. Even so, one suspects that DeBuin's thinking will be concentrated on immediate practical problems, like staying alive, rather than larger questions of what it means to be here in the first place. Although DeBuin's initial questions could not too fancifully be related to King Lear's anguished demand 'What cause in Nature makes these hard hearts?' he is no more likely to find an answer.

In choosing to keep the debate on a moral or philosophical plane, rather than a historical and political one, Aldrich perhaps ensures that this is the case. Certainly in asking why the Apaches behave as they do, their dispossession by the white man does not seem to be a prime factor. 'Is how they are,' Ke-Ni-Tay says of his people, offering a timeless, essentialist explanation. Yet Aldrich in interview said 'Sharp, Lancaster and I totally believed in the parallel with Vietnam' (Coombs 1978: 40). It was intended to be apparent, even though the producer's worries about the effect on the public of an overtly critical view of the war probably worked in the film's favour. In fact the public were confused by the picture, and Aldrich appears to accept responsibility for this confusion. In the summer of 1974 he seemed unaware of the degree of success he had achieved in spite of poor business at the box office: 'In theory it was supposed to be metaphorical. In practice, it wasn't that important' (cited in Coombs 1978: 67). Of course it is not 'King Lear'; both Ulzana and McIntosh are based on stereotypes long familiar in the genre, and their death falls some way short of tragedy. If we see the beginnings of a new relationship between the two young men, DeBuin and Ke-Ni-Tay, their future co-operation and their common home in the cavalry is endowed with little of the social optimism Ford had managed 20 years earlier. Yet one is happy to agree with Nachbar that the film at least demonstrates that in 1972 the conventions and traditions of the western were capable of a new historical perspective, and a thought-provoking blend of action and analysis.

Dances with Wolves

After the spate of films set among the Indians at the beginning of the 1970s, Hollywood moved on to other topics, although *The Outlaw Josey Wales* (1976) did give Chief Dan George an opportunity to capitalise on his success as Old Lodge Skins in *Little Big Man*. It was more than a decade before Kevin Costner's unequivocally sympathetic portrait of the Sioux found favour at the box office, even with audiences who did not see themselves as western buffs. Yet the $18 million project is based on one of the oldest myths of our culture: that it is possible to escape the pressures and complications of modern living for a simpler, more harmonious life. Where Penn's anti-hero moves to and fro between Indians and whites, Costner's Lieutenant Dunbar moves always in the same direction. Where Aldrich's Indians remain irreducibly other, the Plains Indians of *Dances with Wolves* offer unproblematic assimilation.

The film opens in Tennessee in 1863 with the Civil War as a metaphor for the destructive madness of civilisation. Dunbar is about to have his leg amputated when the surgeon's coffee break gives him a chance to remake his destiny. On impulse he mounts up and rides towards the enemy, inviting the bullets but miraculously surviving unscathed. His bizarre gesture has the effect of breaking the stalemate and the Unionists achieve victory: 'In trying to produce my own death I was elevated to the status of a living hero.' This introduces the voice-over, based on the journal Dunbar keeps, which acts as a commentary throughout. The effect is quite unlike the device in Penn's film, where Crabb's sardonic retrospective raises questions and complicates what we are seeing. Dunbar's summary always confirms the visuals, its naïve tone and simple pieties exactly matching the story unfolding before us, although Michael Walker, in a sympathetic account of the film in Cameron & Pye (1996) is perhaps right to remind us that Costner's film is at least more complex than Dunbar's journal.

His foot saved by the general's personal physician, Dunbar is rewarded with a posting of his choice and opts to go west, to Fort Hayes on the prairie. As he explains on arrival, 'I've always wanted to see the frontier ... before it's gone'. The commanding officer is one of the crazed military men familiar from movies of the 1960s, at the end of his tether, his desk full of bottles. Drunkenly he entrusts him to a 'peasant' whose wagon will take him on to Fort Sedgwick, 'the furthest outpost of the realm'. Out on the plains, the heavy wagon and trailer pulled by a team of mules is accompanied by expansive music for the strings and lower brass, a recurring theme which seems never to resolve or progress, but the scenery is breathtaking. One reverse zoom, which slowly reveals the wagon in the surrounding panorama of valley floor, mountains and sky, conveying the sheer scale of the country as only the wide screen can, is worth the admission money in itself.

Where Jack Crabb found it difficult at first to distinguish between the Indian camp and the dump, here it is the white man who has polluted the environment, and Dunbar's first self-assigned duty is to clear up the post, dragging a rotting animal carcass from the water hole and cremating it. The smoke is seen by a party of Indians – not the peaceful Sioux we shall meet later, but the treacherous Pawnee, their shaven heads and grotesque war-paint as terrifying as any screen redskin. Again we have the splitting into 'good' and 'bad' Indians, with the Sioux and the Pawnee cast for the respective roles – as in *Little Big Man*. We can, if we wish, see the 'bad' Indians as created by the white man, their savagery answering to his prejudice; they are hostile because that is how he defines them, but this film is not concerned with the moral debate we meet in *Ulzana's Raid*. Traditionally, cinema audiences have enjoyed being frightened by savages, and Costner is not about to deny us that pleasure.

Dunbar's first encounter with 'a wild Indian' – as he records in his journal – comes a few days later while he is swimming in the water hole, although the meeting ends in comic recoil at the unexpected mutual discovery. That Dunbar is stark naked contributes to this, yet we can see it as another stage in his putting off his white identity in preparation for taking on another. Already he has befriended a solitary wolf which visits the post; relations with animals are a significant motif in this ecological western, Dunbar's fondness for his horse Cisco linking him with the Sioux's dependence on their ponies and the buffalo. In contrast, the whites kill the buffalo just for their tongues and skins. Who would do such a thing, Dunbar asks himself, but 'a people without values and without soul?' Like the wolf, the Sioux are shy creatures, and Dunbar's gradual progress with Two Socks, as he names the wolf, parallels his tentative advances towards the Indians.

We also see the situation from their side since, although Costner chooses to have them speaking throughout in Lakota, their native language, the subtitles enable us to eavesdrop on their councils. The solitary white man is a potential problem because others may follow him. They too have their prejudices: the whites are 'dirty' says Wind in His Hair (Rodney A. Grant), the fierce young brave who provides a contrast with the quieter Kicking Bird (Graham Green), while the old chief Ten Bears (Floyd Red Crow Westerman) reserves judgment: 'It's easy to become confused by these questions'. Ten Bears, 'an extraordinary man' as Dunbar comes to think of him, is not unlike old Lodge Skins, but the mystical side of the Sioux is completely omitted, even though Kicking Bear is introduced as 'a holy man'. Nor do we see much of their daily life apart from a few shots of women dressing buffalo hides, but children are much in evidence, and the womenfolk are allowed their say. 'I'd never known a people so eager to laugh, so devoted to family, so dedicated to each other,' Dunbar will come to realise, although getting to know them will occupy a perhaps disproportionate amount of the film's three hours.

When he decides to take the initiative and pay a visit to the Indian camp he discovers a woman, sheltering beneath a tree, covered in blood. Since we are used to seeing Indian women played by white actresses, it is not immediately apparent that Mary McDonnell, who is to provide the love interest, is in fact a white woman, adopted by the Sioux when a child. The decision to single out Christine, or Stands with a Fist, to give her Indian name, as the object of Dunbar's attention could be seen as a characteristic evasion of the racial issue, but as Kicking Bird's wife puts it, 'It makes sense. They are both white.'

As a sexual partner she combines modesty with the 'pleasing enthusiasm' acclaimed by Lodge Skins, deferring to the man while maintaining a proper self-respect. The origin of her name, awarded because she stood up for herself when bullied by the older women, makes this point, and incidentally offers a rare negative picture of Indian life in reporting the back-breaking toil we never get to see. As usual, Costner balances the opposed nuances with a care that risks debilitating blandness. 'Nothing I have been told about these people is correct,' he confides to his journal as his progress brings growing insight into their customs.

The buffalo are central to the culture of the Plains Indians and the ensuing hunt is one of the film's big set pieces, with convincing use of special effects and moving camera to carry us into the midst of the herd. Dunbar rides with them and gains further kudos when he shoots a huge bull just as it is about to trample an Indian who has fallen from his pony. More spectacular shots of the Indians strung out against the skyline confirm the idyllic journal entries: 'It seems every day ends with a miracle here ... the only word that came to mind was harmony'. Viewers beginning to wilt under the unremitting bliss may think of other words, or wonder how plausible would be the dance Dunbar executes, back at Sedgwick, with the wolf looking on, without the soundtrack's additional backing. That the whole business does not seem even more embarrassingly fey is a tribute to Costner's direction and his simple characterisation of Dunbar, which are all of a piece, leaving no room for condescension or irony.

Dunbar's new identity is to be tried in love and war, and when Kicking Bird and the other braves leave him in charge of the camp he successfully fights off a band of Pawnees. At the climax their leader, who is built up as the villain of the piece, is driven into the river, surrounded and shot down; a spectacular cinematic image which cathartically releases the violence of the encounter.

If self-discovery is the principal theme of the film, then Dunbar's is now complete, only to be confirmed by marriage to Stands with a Fist and rejection by his fellow whites. This comes about when the tribe move on and he remembers the journal he has left behind at the fort, the physical evidence which connects his new life with the old. When he returns to retrieve it he discovers that the army have arrived and some of the troopers, mistaking him for an Indian (he now wears Sioux clothing and feathers in his hair) shoot his horse and take him captive. Recognising that he has turned 'Injun' they offer him a chance to redeem his treachery by leading them to the camp where the 'hostiles' are to be found. He will answer only in Lakota so is put in chains to be taken back to Fort Hayes.

This reversal of the one-way direction of the narrative is short-lived. Although the soldiers amuse themselves by shooting Two Socks, in spite of Dunbar's efforts to save the wolf, the Sioux have seen their friend's arrest and intervene as the column ford a river. The whites are wiped out, Dunbar joining in despite his manacles and drowning one of his tormentors. Again the violence is disturbing and it is registered in the silent alarm of one of the young Indian boys, but ultimately accepted as necessary. Where Jack Crabb was torn between his two identities, albeit mostly subject to the limitations of the comic mode, as Ten Bears sees it: 'The man the soldiers are looking for no longer exists. Now there is only a Sioux named Dances with Wolves'.

Dunbar had come out to the plains in April, and the changing seasons mark the time he spends there. Now it is winter, an opportunity for more handsome photography by Dean Semler as Dances with Wolves and his wife prepare to move on. We cut to the cavalry, moving through the snow guided by a Pawnee scout, and further intercutting between the leave-taking and the advancing troops offers to build tension even at this late stage of an oddly lethargic movie. Perhaps we shall have the kind of massacre perpetrated at Sand Creek or by the Wichita River, even if the protagonists escape. But when the soldiers reach the snow covered riverbank, the camp is deserted, with only a lone wolf howling from the hill. Although Dunbar had said that he must go and 'talk with those who would listen', we know that no action he takes will change the course of history. The inevitability of the processes involved gives the film its curiously muted quality; the Indians may be morally right, but they are still doomed to extinction. The final title, after we see the fur-clad husband and wife moving away from us up among the snow-covered pines, tells us that 13 years later, 'their homes destroyed, their buffalo gone, the last band of free Sioux submitted to white authority at Fort Robinson, Nebraska. The great horse culture of the plains was gone, and the American frontier was soon to pass into history.'

If we can accept Costner's elaborately pictorial account, where even the energy of the competently directed action sequences soon sinks back into the elegiac mood of the whole, then he has marked its passing with appropriate solemnity. How the west was lost is his theme, and it unfolds without bitterness or protest. The success of the film made it easier to finance other Indian projects, like Mann's *The Last of the Mohicans* and Walter Hill's *Geronimo: An American Legend* (1994), the title of the latter suggesting that this time the Native American will be centre stage, a fundamental element in the shaping of the nation rather than simply an obstacle to it. It promises, to borrow the title of a thoughtful essay by Richard Maltby in Cameron & Pye (1996), 'A Better Sense of History'. In his 'Film Diary' (*Sight and Sound*, October 1994: 18) the screenwriter Larry Gross outlines the seriousness of their approach, which he sees as alluding to contemporary tragic events in Yugoslavia and the Middle East, and also the issues of political correctness which dogged the picture; although they are not the peaceful Plains Indians of *Dances with Wolves*, the Apaches cannot now be shown to be too savage. As Geronimo, Wes Studi, the fearsome Pawnee war-chief of Costner's film, is given more of a voice than Ulzana, although here too it is the challenge to liberal white consciousness that structures the story. In the event another holocaust movie, *Schindler's List* (1993), took the Oscars, and unsympathetic reviewers could dismiss the film as having nothing new to say. 'White men speak in forked tongues and Indians are treated shamefully' (*Sight and Sound*, November 1994: 47). This consensus, arrived at over the last 50 years, may be an advance on the captivity narratives of the seventeenth century, but the 'truly meaningful dialogue' with Native American culture which Jon Tuska (1985: 260) hopes for has still to be developed.

6   BREAKING THE MOULD

If the Indian movies of the 1990s were only partially successful in re-imagining traditional accounts of the clash between cultures, they can be seen to form part of a wider revisionist impulse; a logical outcome, Leighton Grist would suggest (Cameron & Pye 1996: 294), of a new political climate ushered in by the Democrats' return to power in 1992. Mario Van Peebles's *Posse* (1993) deserves a mention for promoting black actors, while women began to escape from their sadly constrained roles (although *Johnny Guitar* had already been an exception that proved the rule), sometimes merely fashionably, as in Ruddy, Morgan and Finch's *Bad Girls* (1994), but occasionally more seriously, as in Maggie Greenwald's *The Ballad of Little Jo* (1993).

Yet the most talked-about western of the decade was produced by a man who had graduated from television's *Rawhide* back in the 1960s, via Cinecitta, to create the American action hero – 'cruel, brutal and tall' in Alex Cox's phrase. In the best study of this work of 'cultural production', Paul Smith (1993) sees Eastwood's first Hollywood western *Hang 'Em High* (1968) as the start of a process of restitution, melding the anti-hero of the Dollars pictures with the 'justifiable' violence of the classical phase. The process is continued in *The Outlaw Josey Wales*, for many still his best western, and even more explicitly in *Pale Rider* (1985), which revisits *Shane,* though with a new emphasis on questions of gender and ecology.

When he returns to the form after a gap of seven years, during which he has aged sufficiently to do justice to David Webb Peoples' script, written in the 1970s, like Will Munny he is looking back over his former life and in particular the part that violence has played in it. As Leighton Grist puts it, in a comprehensive essay which accepts the revisionist aspirations of the film, 'the sense of the "return" of Munny's repressed self is underscored by the emergence of Eastwood's familiar persona' (Cameron & Pye 1996: 299). Although he long ago succeeded John Wayne as the genre's archetypal hero, as Amy Taubin argues in reviewing *In the Line of Fire* (1994), 'unlike Wayne, Eastwood does not only embody masculinity, he is also its analyst and critic' (*Sight and Sound*, September 1994: 10). While she is clearly right that the persona is 'riddled with contradictions', whether these contradictions are held in a coherent statement about the relationship of savagery and civilisation is still open to debate.

Unforgiven

The title for Eastwood's tenth western omits the definite article, perhaps to avoid confusion with John Houston's 1959 study of racial prejudice, but perhaps also to diffuse the somewhat puzzling implications of the concept. Who exactly, we wonder, is unforgiven? Is it the two cowboys whose initial cruel action precipitates the narrative – one of whom at least seems in no real sense guilty – or is it rather, as William Munny grimly observes, that 'We all have it coming'? In interview Eastwood claimed that the film was intended as 'a statement about violence and the moral issue of it', the characters bound by the consequences of their behaviour: 'everything they have done is having repercussions' (*Literature/Film Quarterly*, 21, 16). Munny is introduced to us in the opening legend, silhouetted against a red sky and low horizon, as 'a known thief and murderer ... a man of notoriously vicious and intemperate disposition', but when we eventually get to meet him he is doing his best to escape this characterisation, and the stilted phrasing, half comic in effect, and our own familiarity with the Eastwood persona, incline us to doubt that he can be all bad. In appearance at least, as the stranger who rides up to tempt him back to his former ways comments, 'You don't look no meaner-than-hell cold-blooded killer'. Already we have seen the macho hero of the *Dollars* trilogy dragged through the mire by the pigs he is trying to farm, his hair cropped and grizzled, his manner slow and bemused as Eastwood hides none of his 60 years. His reputation has attracted the Schofield Kid, looking for a partner to assist at a killing, but as Munny insists, 'I ain't like that any more'.

Marriage to the now dead Claudia has 'straightened him up', but the need to earn some money to help his son and daughter, coupled with a desire to get back to what he can do well, tempt him to accompany the Kid (Jaimz Woolvett) in exacting retribution for the mutilated whore Delilah (Anna Thompson). En route they call on his former partner Ned Logan (Morgan Freeman), who has also taken up farming with Sally, his Indian wife. The musical score, for the most part muted and unobtrusive, broadens to a pastoral theme, and the natural scene is green and lush. Ned is reluctant to leave it, even when Will reminds him that 'we've done stuff for money before'. But when he embellishes the already exaggerated account of Delilah's injuries given by the Kid, Ned is won over: 'I guess they've got it coming'. The leave-taking, with Sally's wordless reproach as they ride away, is a good example of Eastwood's by now expertly economical direction.

Unlike either of them, we have witnessed the incident in Big Whiskey that has led to the offer of a $1,000 reward which draws them on. The link between sex and violence which runs through the film is established at the outset, when one of the girls, Delilah Fitzgerald, unintentionally mocks the manhood of a customer by giggling at his 'teensy little pecker', and in his drunken fury he slashes her face before his friend or the others can intervene. The sheriff, Little Bill Daggett (Gene Hackman), is summoned, but to the girls' disgust decides on a fine instead of the desired hanging or whipping. His decision to side with Skinny, the proprietor, in seeing it as a matter of 'damaged property', to be settled by compensation in the form of ponies to be delivered when the cowboys return to town in the spring, finds us on the girls' side. Such masculine assumptions are clearly to be questioned, but Little Bill complicates the issue by asking: 'Haven't you seen enough blood for one night?' and suggesting that 'They're just hard-working boys that was foolish', an interpretation the girls have little patience with, hence their decision to raise the money to put up a reward for anyone who will kill those responsible. So revenge, a kind of wild justice, as Bacon called it, motivates the story, but it is less clear-cut than in, say, *The Outlaw Josey Wales*, especially as Delilah's scars begin to heal and those taking revenge have themselves suffered no injury.

The picture's 'deconstructive task' (Harvey Greenberg's phrase from a review in *Film Quarterly*, Spring 1993: 52) is elaborated with the appearance of 'English Bob' (Richard Harris), like Munny and the Schofield Kid attracted by the offered reward. Harris is given some of the picture's rare comedy, and makes the most of it. With W. W. Beauchamp (Saul Rubinek) – his admiring biographer – in tow, he reaches Big Whiskey with lordly disdain for the firearms restrictions Little Bill has imposed. Yet in Bill, an old acquaintance, he has met his match, and is subjected to a fearful kicking, partly the result of the sheriff's natural sadism, partly to warn off others who may disturb the peace by responding to the whores' rumoured reward money.

Beauchamp, whose colourful account of the exploits of 'The Duke of Death' owes something to dime novelist Ned Buntline's mythologising of William Cody as 'Buffalo Bill', raises questions about the relationship between fact and legend, another item in the film's deconstructive project. English Bob, the Duke (or 'the Duck' as Little Bill persists in calling him), has in fact made his mark by shooting 'Chinamen' for the railway, and his exploits are less glamorous than the legend implies. The themes of sex and violence and fact and legend come together in Bill's revisionist account of one such exploit in a Wichita saloon which he witnessed – the shooting of Two-Gun Corcoran. The nickname, it transpires, is not derived from his armament but the fact that 'his dick was so big it was longer than the barrel on the Walker Colt he carried'. In the bungled, drunken duel with Bob the Colt exploded, leaving him at the other man's mercy. As Bill explains: 'If he had two guns instead of just a big dick he would have been right there to the end to defend himself'.

The clichéd symbol of gun as phallus gets a further twist when, after more humiliation in the gaol Bob is turned loose, his six-gun returned to him bent into an absurdly detumescent droop. The idea is again shadowily present as the Schofield Kid (who takes his name from the Smith and Wesson Colt he carries) proves unable to hit anything with his rifle, while angrily denying Ned's suggestion that 'something might be bent'. In fact the reason is his poor eyesight – but then blindness too is a figure for impotence, and for all his big talk, the Kid's immaturity makes him less than a man. Not that he fails to perform with the women. When disillusioned with Will's defeat by Little Bill he claims that at least he would have pulled his pistol, Ned answers, 'Well, you did – right out of the lady and out of the Goddamned window'. In the final sequence Will arms himself with both the Kid's pistol and Ned's rifle, back – as Eastwood puts it – 'in full possession of his abilities'.

Out on the trail the Kid provides a parallel to Beauchamp, each avid for details of his hero's past deeds, but Will claims he 'don't recollect', unhappy to be reminded of the deaths he has caused. Unable to rewrite history to justify his deeds, his conscience increasingly troubles him. In particular he remembers a drover he shot through the mouth: 'I think about him now and again ... he didn't do anything to deserve to get shot'. What he is looking for is confirmation that he has changed: 'I'm just a fellow now. I ain't no different than anyone else no more'. The internal conflict, as much as the pouring rain, seems to account for the feverish sickness which afflicts him, so that he is powerless to resist Bill's bullying when they do eventually reach Big Whiskey and the billiards hall, and so suffers the same fate as English Bob.

Eastwood draws attention to the similarity between Will and Bill, although the latter has the advantage in that his violence is legitimised by his office. Each is trying to make a new life, symbolised in the house Bill is building for himself, where he looks forward to sitting on the porch, smoking his pipe and watching the sun go down. If Munny is unsuccessful as a pig farmer, his stock sickening and dying, Little Bill – in his deputy's opinion – is 'the worst damn carpenter', his roof scarcely serving to keep out the rain that has soaked Will to the skin. We first see him hitting his thumb with a hammer, a comically simple metaphor for his ineptitude. Yet he is a figure of power, ruling over his bunch of deputies with easy superiority, a stranger to inner doubt. Unselfishly Eastwood gives Hackman space to elaborate the role of outlaw-turned-lawman, a familiar one in the genre, and the actor turns in another excellent performance: 'I tried to make him human and a monster at the same time' (*Literature/Film Quarterly*, 21, 16).

When, after three days, the fever breaks, Will wakes to see Delilah. The snow-covered countryside has a welcoming freshness, and for one of the few sequences in an overwhelmingly under-lit film we see the sun. She offers him 'a free one', as his friends have both been anticipating the reward in the form of sexual favours, but memories of Claudia hold him back. The simple guitar theme heard over the opening titles resurfaces, perhaps connected with the dear departed, who he tells Delilah is in Kansas, 'watching over my young ones'. Romance is a possibility: 'You ain't ugly like me,' he reassures her, 'it's just that we've both got scars'. Like Ford's Ringo and Dallas, the outlaw and prostitute might make a new life together. One wonders about her name; beneath her meek exterior, is she another castrating female, to deflect him from his task? In fact she tells him that the reward money is still on offer. The solidarity of the women, in asserting their worth in the face of masculine ill-treatment, strikes us as a positive note, although we never forget that they are as unforgiving as anyone. When the young cowboy brings an extra pony for Delilah, in addition to the two promised to Skinny, there is a prolonged pause while they wonder how to react, but when they do it is with a shower of stones and insults, his offer indignantly rejected.

The impossibility of a change of direction, in spite of the sweet music and Delilah's feminine softness, is savagely emphasised with the cut that takes us from the relaxed moment, with Will savouring the beauties of the world he thought he was about to leave, to the ambush of the same young cowboy, Davey, who had tried to make amends. The horror of the scene is brought out by the Kid's repeated questioning as his defective eyesight prevents him seeing what is happening. 'We killed him – I guess,'

Will eventually admits, and calls down to Davey's friends to take him the water he is crying for.

When the news reaches town, the women are unrepentant. 'He had it coming,' Strawberry Alice shouts back, while Will leaves the Kid to make the other killing (his first, as it unsurprisingly turns out) when they stake out the remaining culprit, Quick Mike. Foul-mouthed and overconfident, he attracts none of the sympathy elicited by Davey, but even so his death – he is grotesquely dispatched while sitting in the outhouse lavatory – is shocking. Whatever glamour the gunfighter's life might have is finally over. 'Is that what it was like in the old days, Will?' the Kid asks, bravado struggling with his tears. 'I can't remember. I was drunk most of the time.' For once in the film Will is moved to sententiousness: 'It's a helluva thing, killing a man. You take away all he's got, and all he's ever going to have.' While the Kid clings to the notion of justification, with the usual tag, 'I guess he had it coming', Will seems to find the distinction irrelevant. Yet he is visibly disturbed when with a further irony together with the reward money, delivered as arranged by one of the prostitutes, comes news of Ned's death at the hands of Little Bill. Earlier we have seen the Negro tied to the cell bars, his back whipped raw. As portrayed by Morgan Freeman he is perhaps the most sympathetic character in the story, and as with most of the violent scenes, there is little kinetic excitement – no one ever fights back – the reaction of the spectators present (in particular here W. W. Beauchamp, who winces at each lash) obliging us to suffer the pain without relief.

Eastwood has spoken of Will's reverting to his violent ways as though 'a kind of machinery was back in action' (*Literature/Film Quarterly*, 21, 11). The pretence of being 'just a fellow' is abandoned, and we hear no further mention of Claudia as he reached for the whisky bottle to take his first drink in ten years. The Kid – like Will's comrades in his former life – now afraid of him, recognises the difference: 'I ain't like you, Will.' In Will Wright's classification of the classical western, 'the society recognises a difference between themselves and the hero; the hero is given a special status' (1975: 168). Now provided with an 'honourable' motive, retribution for his 'innocent' friend's death, the hero rides into town for the final gun-down. Lennie Niehaus's music becomes still more minimalist, reduced to a few sinister sustained chords as we see the wet street from Will's point of view, hunched over his horse through the rain and darkness, past the open coffin outside Greely's where Ned's body is displayed.

Inside, Little Bill is addressing his posse, when – as though in tribute to Sergio Leone (the film is dedicated 'to Sergio and Don') – a shotgun enters the frame. Thunder rumbles as the conversation dies: 'Who's the fellow owns this shit-hole?' When Skinny comes forward he is shot down without compunction, and there is even a hint of the ironic comedy of the spaghettis as Will replies to Bill's 'Well sir, you're a cowardly son of a bitch. You've just killed an unarmed man.' 'He should have armed himself if he was going to decorate his saloon with my friend,' comes the reply. Whereas earlier he had tried to escape the legend, now he borrows its rhetoric in a commentary on his own actions: 'I've killed just about everything that walks or crawls at one time or another. I'm here to kill you, Little Bill, for what you did to Ned.' Bill's courage is not in doubt, and when the shotgun's second barrel misfires he tries to take his chance, but Will guns him down and three of his deputies with the Kid's Schofield, remaining unscathed himself. Bill is in fact not dead, but Will kicks aside his raised gun and levels Ned's rifle at his throat. 'I don't deserve this. To die like this,' Bill protests, 'I was building a house.' 'Deserve's got nothing to do with it,' Will counters, also kicking aside the simple morality of the traditional western. In the long pause as he sights along the barrel before pulling the trigger, his expression is inscrutable.

Where before, as if lacking a language of his own, he had mouthed Claudia's pious platitudes, not altogether convincingly, he now takes his cue from the highly coloured prose of the kind of novel Beachamp might write, to dramatise his determination: 'All right, I'm coming out. Any son-of-a-bitch takes a shot at me I'm going to kill him ... I'm going to kill his wife, all his friends. Burn his damn house down.' He rides off into the darkness with a glance back at Ned's body and further advice to the silently watching townsfolk not 'to cut up nor otherwise harm no whores. Or I'll come back and kill every one of you sons-of-bitches.'

The closing legend, which recapitulates the opening shot of the cabin silhouetted against the red sky, shows us that he returned home, then disappeared. When his mother-in-law comes out to Kansas, she can find no sign of him, nor any indication why her daughter should have married 'a known thief and murderer'. The teasing enigma remains, and the film's ending continues to divide the critics. Len Dobbs thinks we 'exit the theatre in elation that things are as they used to be' (*Sight and Sound*, October 1992: 16), having witnessed the hero rediscover his true metier, and released through violence, free to move on into the future. But to accept this 'happy ending' we have to discount a good deal of what has gone before. Although structurally Little Bill may be the villain, responsible for the death of the hero's friend, he has his humanities, and as Harvey Greenberg notes, he did at least hold things together; it is hard to believe that society will be safer for his demise. The legend's account of a subsequent normal life for the protagonist thus becomes deeply equivocal, 'softening into more "acceptable" obscurity the baleful spectacle of Munny's frightening rehabilitation' (*Film Quarterly*, Spring 1993: 56). Perhaps Will's reported success in the dry goods line is confirmation that 'deserve's got nothing to do with it'; perhaps his iconic power takes him beyond any just distribution of rewards and punishments. 'A man has to be what he is ... you can't break the mould. I tried it and it didn't work for me.' Shane's last words could equally apply here, forty years on.

More harshly, in Maggie Greenwald's opinion, 'it's the same old stuff' (Kitses & Rickman 1998: 365). But surely Will's legacy to the Kid is not like Shane's to Joey, a role model to help him grow up 'strong and straight', but a frightening warning of the dehumanising effects of the life he has followed. We can perhaps take comfort, Grist suggests (Cameron & Pye 1996: 301), in the marginal figures – Davey, Delilah, and the Kid – who may be able to construct a different kind of future, but the disturbing final impression is of 'the fiction returning in overpowering form to literally blow away the demythologising truthfulness of the sheriff' (Smith 1993: 268). The fiction, the myth of the indestructible hero, is not yet exhausted.

Space is the final frontier, and for his latest project, *Space Cowboys* (2000), Eastwood assembles other veterans to take on a malfunctioning Russian satellite, but only its title and the fact — relevant perhaps to its decline — that the western has traditionally privileged maturity and experience, connect it with the genre where he made his name. It is unlikely that we shall see him saddle up again, or that the western will ever occupy a central place in our film-going experience, for Kitses and Rickman a part of the postmodern condition and not something to be mourned. Their enthusiasm for the form — when so many of its adherents have accepted the inevitability of its decline — is heartwarming, but to claim that the westerns of the 1990s prove it 'gloriously alive' (1998: 16) is to take the wish for the deed. If *Unforgiven* is to remain the last truly memorable western, we shall have to make do with the rapidly growing body of criticism to which the collections by Cameron and Pye and Kitses and Rickman have notably contributed, and take comfort that there are few weeks when one of the television channels does not remind us of the long history of the form, and few years when at least some of the films discussed in this book do not appear on the small screen.

FILMOGRAPHY

Apache (Robert Aldrich, 1954, US)

Apocalypse Now (Francis Coppola, 1979, US)

Bad Girls (Charles Finch, Andre Morgan, Albert S. Ruddy, 1994, US)

The Ballad of Billy Jo (Maggie Greenwald, 1993, US)

Ballad of Cable Hogue, The (Sam Peckinpah, 1969, US)

Bend of the River (Anthony Mann, 1952, US)

Blazing Saddles (Mel Brooks, 1974, US)

Bonnie and Clyde (Arthur Penn, 1967, US)

Broken Arrow (Delmer Daves, 1950, US)

Broken Lance (Sol Siegel, 1954, US)

Butch Cassidy and the Sundance Kid (George Roy Hills, 1969, US)

Cat Ballou (Elliot Silverstein, 1965, US)

Chato's Land (Michael Winner, 1971, UK)

Cheyenne Autumn (John Ford, 1964, US)

The Covered Wagon (James Cruze, 1923, US)

Dances With Wolves (Kevin Costner, 1990, US)

Dead Man (Jim Jarmusch, 1996, US)

Death Wish (Michael Winner, 1974, US)

Dodge City (Michael Curtiz, 1939, US)

Dr Strangelove (Stanley Kubrick, 1963, GB)

Drums Along the Mohawk (John Ford, 1939, US)

El Dorado (Howard Hawks, 1966, US)

The Far Country (Anthony Mann, 1954, US)

Fistful of Dollars, A/Per un pugno di dollari (Sergio Leone, 1964, It.)

Fort Apache (John Ford, 1948, US)

Four for Texas (Robert Aldrich, 1963, US)

Geronimo: An American Legend (Walter Hill, 1994, US)

The Good, the Bad and the Ugly/Il buono, il brutto, il cattivo (Sergio Leone, 1966, It.)

The Grapes of Wrath (John Ford, 1940, US)

The Great Northfield Minnesota Raid (Philip Kaufman, 1972, US)

The Great Train Robbery (Edwin S. Porter, 1903, US)

The Gunfighter (Henry King, 1950, US)

Hang 'Em High (Ted Post, 1968, US)

High Noon (Fred Zinnemann, 1952, US)

High Plains Drifter (Clint Eastwood, 1972, US)

How the West Was Won (John Ford, Henry Hathaway, George Marshall, 1962, US)

In the Line of Fire (Clint Eastwood, 1994, US)

The Iron Horse (John Ford, 1924, US)

The James Boys in Missouri (Jesse James Jr, 1908, US)

Jesse James (Henry King, 1939, US)

Johnny Guitar (Nicholas Ray, 1954, US)

The Last of the Mohicans (Michael Mann, 1992, US)

The Left-Handed Gun (Arthur Penn, 1958, US)

Little Big Man (Arthur Penn, 1970, US)

Lonely Are the Brave (David Miller, 1962, US)

The Long Riders (Walter Hill, 1980, US)

The Magnificent Seven (John Sturges, 1960, US)

Major Dundee (Sam Peckinpah, 1964, US)

A Man Called Horse (Elliot Silverstein, 1970, US)

The Man from Laramie (Anthony Mann, 1955, US)

Man of the West (Anthony Mann, 1958, US)

The Man Who Shot Liberty Valance (John Ford, 1962, US)

The Missouri Breaks (Arthur Penn, 1976, US)

My Darling Clementine (John Ford, 1946, US)

My Name is Nobody (Tonino Valerii, 1973, It.)

The Naked Spur (Anthony Mann, 1952, US)

Once Upon a Time in the West/C'era una volta il west (Sergio Leone, 1968, It.)

One-Eyed Jacks (Marlon Brando, 1961, US)

Only Angels Have Wings (Howard Hawks, 1939, US)

The Outlaw Josey Wales (Clint Eastwood, 1976, US)

Pale Rider (Clint Eastwood, 1985, US)

Pat Garrett and Billy the Kid (Sam Peckinpah, 1973, US)

Posse (Mario Van Peebles, 1993, US)

The Professionals (Richard Brooks, 1966, US)

Rebel Without a Cause (Nicholas Ray, 1955, US)

Red River (Howard Hawks, 1948, US)

Reservoir Dogs (Quentin Tarantino, 1992, US)

The Return of Frank James (Fritz Lang, 1940, US)

Ride the High Country/Guns in the Afternoon (Sam Peckinpah, 1962, US)

Rio Bravo (Howard Hawks, 1959, US)

Rio Lobo (Howard Hawks, 1970, US)

Schindler's List (Steven Spielberg, 1993, US)

The Searchers (John Ford, 1956, US)
The Seven Samurai (Akira Kurosawa, 1954, Japan)
Shane (George Stevens, 1953, US)
She Wore a Yellow Ribbon (John Ford, 1949, US)
Soldier Blue (Ralph Nelson, 1970, US)
Space Cowboys (Clint Eastwood, 2000, US)
Stagecoach (John Ford, 1939, US)
Tell Them Willie Boy is Here (Abraham Polonsky, 1969, US)
They Died With Their Boots On (Raoul Walsh, 1941, US)
Tombstone (George P. Cosmatos, 1993, US)
True Grit (Henry Hathaway, 1969, US)
Ulzana's Raid (Robert Aldrich, 1972, US)
Unforgiven (Clint Eastwood, 1992, US)
The Unforgiven (John Houston, 1959, US)
Vera Cruz (Robert Aldrich, 1954, US)
Wagon Master (John Ford, 1959, US)
The Wild Bunch (Sam Peckinpah, 1969, US)
Will Penny (Tom Gries, 1967, US)
Winchester '73 (Anthony Mann, 1950, US)
Wyatt Earp (Lawrence Kasdan, 1994, US)
Wyatt Earp, Frontier Marshal (Stuart Lake, 1931, US)
Yojimbo (Akira Kurosawa, 1961, Japan)
Young Mr Lincoln (John Ford, 1939, US)

BIBLIOGRAPHY

The bibliography lists works cited in the text and is also designed to point to useful further reading. The annotated list of 'essential reading' highlights works of particular interest, although many valuable contributions are also to be found under 'secondary reading'.

ESSENTIAL READING

Buscombe, Edward (ed.) (1988) *The BFI Companion to the Western*. London: Andre Deutsch.
Encyclopaedic, fully illustrated guide not only to the films and film-makers but the cultural and historical background; includes television westerns and appendices with annual release figures.

Cameron, Ian & Douglas Pye (eds) (1996) *The Movie Book of the Western*. London: Studio Vista.
Thirty articles by different hands covering individual films and more theoretical issues, reflecting recent interest in questions of gender, race and class.

Cawelti, John G. (1971) *The Six-Gun Mystique*. Bowling Green: Bowling Green University Popular Press.
Book-length essay investigating the essence of the western as cultural phenomenon and artistic creation.

Frayling, Christopher (1981) *Spaghetti Westerns: Cowboys and Europeans from Karl May to Sergio Leone*. London: Routledge & Kegan Paul.
Definitive study of the Italian western, but also stimulating on the form in general.

Kitses, Jim (1969) *Horizons West*. Bloomington: Indiana University Press.
Divided between an auteurist study of Mann, Boetticher and Peckinpah and an influential analysis of the structuring oppositions of the genre.

Kitses, Jim & Gregg Rickman (eds) (1998) *The Western Reader*. New York: Limelight.
Reprints some of the pioneering essays on the form but also gives sustained attention to recent revisionist westerns.

Tompkins, Jane (1992) *West of Everything: the Inner Life of Westerns.* New York: Oxford University Press.
Gender-oriented study, seeing the genre in fiction and film as offering models of masculinity in opposition to the dominant domestic tradition of American Victorian culture.

Tuska, Jon (1985) *The American West in Film: Critical Approaches to the Western.* Westport: Greenwood Press.
Difficult to argue with someone who claims to have seen every surviving western film, although some of the opinions provoke disagreement.

Warshow, Robert (1954) 'Movie Chronicle: The Westerner', *Partisan Review,* March–April, re-printed in Kitses & Rickman (1998), 35–47.
Classic essay on the western hero as 'the last gentleman', an archaic figure in a timeless and self-contained drama.

Wright, Will (1975) *Sixguns and Society: A Structural Study of the Western.* Berkeley: University of California Press.
A structuralist account, attempting to relate the genre to the society which consumes it. Often attacked for its reductive analysis, but still relevant and readable.

SECONDARY READING

Anderson, Lindsay (1981) *About John Ford...* London: Plexus.

Bazin, Andre (1971) *What is Cinema? Vol. 2.* Berkeley: University of California Press.

Bogdanovich, Peter (1967) *John Ford.* London: Studio Vista.

Bordwell, David, Janet Staiger & Kristin Thompson (1985) *The Classical Hollywood Cinema: Film Style and Mode of Production to 1960.* New York: University of Columbia Press.

Braudy, Leo (1971) 'The Difficulties of *Little Big Man*', *Film Quarterly,* 25, 30–3.

Buscombe, Edward (1970) 'The Idea of Genre in the American Cinema', *Screen,* 11, 2.

Buscombe, Edward & Roberta E. Pearson (1998) *Back in the Saddle Again: New Essays on the Western.* London: BFI.

Butler, Terence (1979) *Crucified Heroes: The Films of Sam Peckinpah.* London: Gordon Fraser.

Calder, Jenni (1974) *There Must Be a Lone Ranger.* London: Hamish Hamilton.

Carroll, Noel (1998) 'The Professional Western: South of the Border', in Buscombe & Pearson (1998) 46–62.

Coombs, Richard (ed.) (1978) *Robert Aldrich.* London: BFI.

Countryman, Edward & Evonne von Heussen Countryman (1999) *Shane.* London: BFI.

Coyne, Michael (1979) *The Crowded Prairie: American National Identity in the Hollywood Western.* London: I. B. Tauris.

Dobbs, Len (1992) 'Homage to Peckinpah', *Sight and Sound,* 2, 10, 16.

Fenin, George N. & William K. Everson (1977) *The Western: From Silents to the Seventies.* Harmondsworth: Penguin.

Folsom, James K. (1970) '*Shane* and *Hud*: Two Stories in Search of a Medium', *Western Humanities Review,* 1970, 24, reprinted in Pilkington and Graham (1979), 65–80.

French, Philip (1974) *Westerns: Aspects of a Movie Genre.* London: Secker & Warburg.

Friar, Ralph E. and Natasha A. (1972) *The Only Good Indian ... The Hollywood Gospel.* New York: Drama Book Specialists.

Gallagher, Tag (1986) *John Ford: The Man and His Films*. Berkeley: University of California Press.

Grant, Barry K. (ed.) (1986) *Film Genre Reader*. Austin: University of Texas Press.

Gross, Larry (1994) 'Film Diary', *Sight and Sound*, 4, 10, 18.

Hillier, Jim & Peter Wollen (eds) (1996) *Howard Hawks: American Artist*. London: BFI.

Lenihan, John H. (1980) *Showdown: Confronting Modern America in the Western Film*. Urbana and Chicago: University of Illinois Press.

Linet, Beverly (1979) *Ladd: The Life, the Legend and the Legacy of Alan Ladd*. London: Robson Books.

McBride, Joseph (1982) *Hawks on Hawks*. Berkeley: University of California Press.

McBride, Joseph and Michael Wilmington (1975) *John Ford*. New York: Da Capo Press.

Mellen, Joan (1978) *Big Bad Wolves: Masculinity in the American Film*. London: Elm Tree.

Mitchell, Lee Clark (1996) *Westerns: Making the Man in Fiction and Film*. Chicago: University of Chicago Press.

Nachbar, Jack (ed.) (1974) *Focus on the Western*. Englewood Cliffs, NJ: Prentice-Hall.

Nash Smith, Henry (1950) *Virgin Land: The American West as Symbol and Myth*. New York: Vintage.

Pilkington, William T. and Don Graham (eds) (1979) *Western Movies*. Alberquerque: University of New Mexico Press.

Pym, John (1980) Review of *The Long Riders*, *Sight and Sound*, Autumn, 267.

Seydor, Paul (1980) *Peckinpah: The Western Films*. Urbana and Chicago: University of Illinois Press.

Smith, Paul (1993) *Clint Eastwood: A Cultural Production*. London: UCL.

Taubin, Amy (1994) Review of *In the Line of Fire*, *Sight and Sound*, 4, 9, 10.

Thomas, Deborah (2001) *Reading Hollywood: Spaces and Meanings in American Film*. London: Wallflower Press.

Thomson, David (1975) *A Biographical Dictionary of the Cinema*. London: Secker & Warburg.

Turner, Frederick Jackson (1893) 'The Significance of the Frontier in American History', reprinted in Ray Allen Billington (ed) *Frontier and Section: Selected Essays of Frederick Jackson Turner*. Englewood Cliffs: Prentice-Hall, 1961.

Turner, John W. (1977) '*Little Big Man*, the Novel and the Film' *Literature/Film Quarterly* 5 (Spring 1977), reprinted in Pilkington and Graham (1979) 109–122.

Tuska, Jon (1976) *The Filming of the West*. New York: Doubleday.

Weddle, David (1994) *"If they move... Kill 'Em!": The Life and Times of Sam Peckinpah*. New York: Grove Press.

Willis, Donald (1975) *The Films of Howard Hawks*. Metuchen, NJ: Scarecrow.

Wills, Garry (1998) *John Wayne: The Politics of Celebrity*. London: Faber & Faber.

Wollen, Peter (1969) *Signs and Meaning in the Cinema*. London: Secker & Warburg.

Wood, Robin (1968) *Howard Hawks*. London: Secker & Warburg.

Wright, Judith Hess (1974) 'Genre Films and the Status Quo', *Jump Cut* No,1. reprinted in Grant (1986) 41–49.

THE SHORT CUTS SERIES

A comprehensive library of introductory texts covering the full spectrum of Film Studies, specifically designed for building an individually styled library for all students and enthusiasts of cinema and popular culture.

"This series is tailor-made for a modular approach to film studies ... an indispensable tool for both lecturers and students"

01   THE HORROR GENRE
FROM BEELZEBUB TO BLAIR WITCH
Paul Wells

The inaugral book in the Short Cuts series is a comprehensive introduction to the history and key themes of the horror genre. The main issues and debates raised by horror, and the approaches and theories that have been applied to horror texts are all addressed. In charting the evolution of the horror film in social and cultural context, Paul Wells explores how it has reflected and commented upon particular historical periods, and asks how it may respond to the new millennium by citing recent innovations in the genre's development, such as the 'urban myth' narrative underpinning *Candyman* and *The Blair Witch Project*.

"An informed and highly readable account that is theoretically broad, benefiting from a wide range of cinematic examples."

1-903364-00-0   144 pp.

02 THE STAR SYSTEM
HOLLYWOOD'S PRODUCTION OF POPULAR IDENTITIES
Paul McDonald

The Star System looks at the development and changing organization of the star system in the American film industry. Tracing the popularity of star performers from the early 'cinema of attractions' to the internet universe, Paul McDonald explores the ways in which Hollywood has made and sold its stars. Through focusing on particular historical periods, the key conditions influencing the star system in silent cinema, the studio era and the New Hollywood are discussed and illustrated by cases studies of Mary Pickford, Bette Davis, James Cagney, Julia Roberts, Tom Cruise, and Will Smith.

"A very good introduction to the topic filling an existing gap in the needs of researchers and students of the subject."

Roberta Pearson, University of Wales, Cardiff

1-903364-02-7   144 pp.

03 SCIENCE FICTION CINEMA
FROM OUTERSPACE TO CYBERSPACE
Geoff King and Tanya Krzywinska

Science Fiction Cinema charts the dimensions of one of the most popular film genres. From lurid comic-book blockbusters to dark dystopian visions, science fiction is seen as both a powerful cultural barometer of our times and the product of particular industrial and commercial frameworks. The authors outline the major themes of the genre, from representations of the mad scientist and computer hacker to the relationship between science fiction and postmodernism, exploring issues such as the meaning of special effects and the influence of science fiction cinema on the entertainment media of the digital age.

"The best overview of English-language science fiction cinema published to date... thorough, clearly written and full of excellent examples. Highly recommended."

Steve Neale, Sheffield Hallam University

1-903364-03-5   144 pp.

04   EARLY SOVIET CINEMA
INNOVATION. IDEOLOGY AND PROPAGANDA.
David Gillespie

Early Soviet Cinema examines the aesthetics of Soviet cinema during its 'golden age' of the 1920s, against a background of cultural ferment and the construction of a new socialist society. Separate chapters are devoted to the work of Sergei Eisenstein, Lev Kuleshov, Vsevolod Pudovkin, Dziga Vertov and Alexander Dovzhenko. Other major directors are also discussed at length. David Gillespie places primary focus on the text, with analysis concentrating on the artistic qualities, rather than the political implications, of each film. The result is not only a discussion of each director's contribution to the 'golden age' and to world cinema, but also an exploration of their own distinctive poetics.

"An excellent book ... Lively and informative, it fills a significant gap and deserves to be on reading lists wherever courses on Soviet cinema are run."

Graham Roberts, University of Surrey

1-903364-04-3   128 pp.

05   READING HOLLYWOOD
SPACES AND MEANINGS IN AMERICAN FILM
Deborah Thomas

Reading Hollywood examines the treatment of space and narrative in a selection of classic films including *It's A Wonderful life*, *My Darling Clementine* and *Vertigo*. Deborah Thomas employs a variety of arguments in exploring the reading of space and its meaning in Hollywood cinema, and film generally. Topics covered include the importance of space in defining genre (such as the necessity of an urban landscape for a gangster film to be a gangster film), the ambiguity of offscreen space and spectatorship (how an audience reads an unseen but inferred setting), and the use of spatilly disruptive cinematic techniques to construct meaning.

"Among the finest introductions to Hollywood in particular and film studies in general ... subtler, more complex, yet more readable than most of its rivals, many of which it will displace."

Ed Buscombe, editor of *The BFI Companion to the Western*

1-903364-01-9   144 pp.

06   DISASTER MOVIES
THE CINEMA OF CATASTROPHE
Stephen Keane

Disaster Movies provides a comprehensive introduction to the history and development of the disaster genre. The 1950s sci-fi B-movies to high concept 1990s 'millennial movies', Stephen Keane looks at the ways in which the representation of disaster and its aftermath are borne out of both contextual considerations and the increasing commercial demands of contemporary Hollywood. Through detailed analyses of such films as *Airport*, *The PoseidonAdventure*, *Independence Day* and *Titanic*, the book explores the continual reworking of this, to-date, undervalued genre.

"Providing detailed consideration of key movies within their social and cultural context, this concise introduction serves its purpose well and should prove a useful teaching tool."

Nick Roddick

1-903364-05-1   144 pp.

07   NEW CHINESE CINEMA
CHALLENGING REPRESENTATIONS
Sheila Cornelius

New Chinese Cinema examines the 'search for roots' films that emerged from China in the aftermath of the Cultural Revolution. Sheila Cornelius contextualises the films of the so-called 'Fifth Generation' directors who came to prominence in the 1980s and 1990s, such as Chen Kaige, Zhang Yimou and Tian Zhuangzhuan. Including close analysis of such pivotal films as *Farewell My Concubine*, *Raise the Red Lantern* and *The Blue Kite*, the book also examines the rise of contemporary 'Sixth Generation' underground directors whose themse embrace the disaffection of urban youth.

"Very thorough in its coverage of the historical and cultural background to New Chinese Cinema ... clearly written and appropriately targeted at an undergraduate audience."

Leon Hunt, Brunel University

1-903364-13-2   144 pp.